The Cat Who... Cookbook

Julie Murphy
&
Sally Abney Stempinski

Berkley Prime Crime, New York

THE CAT WHO . . . COOKBOOK

A Berkley Prime Crime Book
Published by The Berkley Publishing Group,
a division of Penguin Putnam Inc.,
375 Hudson Street
New York, New York 10014

Design by Pauline Neuwirth, Neuwirth & Associates, Inc.

ISBN 0-425-17674-6

Printed in the United States of America

A Special Note to the Reader

At last! A cookbook with a sense of humor, as well as great recipes from cooks and restaurants in Moose County and Down Below.

At last! We learn the secret of Mrs. Cobb's meat loaf and macaroni and cheese.

At last! Qwilleran may be inspired to try his hand at food preparation. He'll start with—guess what!

Lilian Jackson Braun

This cookbook is dedicated to our supportive family:
Davis, Olivia, Elyse, Nickie, Diane, Steve, and Billy,
who were willing to eat unusual meals—such as three salads
and two desserts on one evening, or two meats and two soups
the next evening—as we tested our recipes;
and to our friends, who gave us
so much encouragement.

Contents

Introduction

For years we have all enjoyed the literary feast of the *Cat Who . . .* novels by Lilian Jackson Braun. Now her books can be the start of a literal feast with the recipes included in this companion cookbook. As tempting as the descriptions of the foods are in the pages of the books, you'll find them even more delectable when you sample them firsthand. Prepare one of Qwilleran's favorite meals and invite friends over to share in the fun and good food. As you write the invitations, ask your guests who are *Cat Who . . .* devotees to come as their favorite character from the book you've selected. A reading of excerpts from the book in which the foods are mentioned is interesting and entertaining.

Perhaps you'll want to set the stage by re-creating a particular scene—serving in front of your fireplace on a table "laid with a dazzling display of porcelain, crystal, and silver" as in *The Cat Who Knew Shakespeare.* Planks "laid across columns of concrete blocks to form a long narrow table" with a centerpiece of "white carnations arranged with weeds," as Courtney had in *The Cat Who Lived High,* is sure to create a memorable experience for your guests. Make tuna sandwiches and brownies and go birding on the banks of a river as Polly and Qwill did in *The Cat Who Knew a Cardinal.* Use this *Cat Who . . . Cookbook* as a start for your own inventive party ideas.

All recipes in this book have been selected to represent the setting of the story, time period within which the book was written, and the character in the story who is preparing the meal. Cooking has changed greatly during the three decades that span the time of the *Cat Who . . .* novels. Consequently, some of the recipes include ingredients that may seem rich or heavy by today's standards. Try the recipe as is, or substitute lighter ingredients to suit your own taste or dietary requirements. Or to save time, substitute commercially prepared piecrusts instead of making your own.

Each section of this companion cookbook begins with a menu for a complete meal found in the corresponding *Cat Who . . .* novel. These were the foods eaten by Qwilleran and his companions.

Following each menu section is the À La Carte section. This section contains individual listings of foods and beverages that are not part of a particular meal, but were ordered or served to Qwilleran and his friends. Try complete menus or mix and match to create your own meals. The index in the back will assist in planning a *Cat Who . . .* feast from several novels.

We can't forget food for the pampered pet. Like clockwork, Koko and Yum Yum expect their dinners, too. The "catcipes" listed in the Feline Fare section are some of Koko and Yum Yum's favorite repasts—crabmeat garnished with goat cheese or sautéed chicken livers with a garnish of egg yolk and bacon crumbles. With a few meals like these, perhaps your own feline friends will amaze you with some detective work of their own.

Bon appetit!

The Cat Who Could Read Backwards

Qwilleran acquires a Siamese cat named Kao K'o-Kung, aka Koko, under unusual circumstances. Perhaps it would be more accurate to say Koko acquires a human named Qwilleran, aka a journalist. Together they solve a murder in the world of modern art.

Mountclemens's Dinner

Lobster Bisque

❦

Chicken in a Dark and Mysterious Sauce

❦

Caesar Salad

❦

Chocolate Mousse

"We've got news for you, Jim. We called Mountclemens to make an appointment for you, and he wants you to go tomorrow night. To dinner!" ...

"And now I believe we are ready for the soup." [said Mountclemens] *The critic drew aside some dark red velvet curtains. An aroma of* **lobster** *greeted Qwilleran in the dining alcove. Plates of soup, thick and creamy, were placed on a bare table that looked hundreds of years old. Thick candles burned in iron holders.*

Lobster Bisque

½ cup chopped onion
½ cup chopped celery
3 tablespoons butter or margarine
3 tablespoons all-purpose flour
¼ teaspoon nutmeg
3 cups milk
1 bay leaf
1 boiled lobster or 2 small boiled lobster tails cut into bite-sized chunks
2 cups cream
salt and pepper to taste
4 tablespoons sherry

Sauté the onion and celery in the butter or margarine until tender. Add flour and nutmeg. Stir well. Add the milk, stirring constantly. Then add the bay leaf. Cook, stirring, until the mixture thickens. Reduce the heat. Add the lobster, cream, salt, pepper, and sherry. Heat but do not boil again. Remove the bay leaf. SERVES 4–6.

Mountclemens removed the soup plates and brought in a tureen of **chicken in a dark and mysterious sauce.**

Chicken in a Dark and Mysterious Sauce

———————

4–6   chicken breasts
all-purpose flour to coat chicken
3   tablespoons butter or margarine
2   tablespoons cooking oil
salt and pepper to taste
4   tablespoons all-purpose flour
½   teaspoon cinnamon
2   14½–ounce cans chicken broth
½   ounce melted unsweetened baking chocolate
⅓   cup chopped onion
¾   cup chopped carrots
½   cup raisins
½   cup sliced almonds for garnish (optional)

Preheat oven to 325°. Dredge chicken with flour until well-covered. Brown chicken in butter or margarine and oil. Season with salt and pepper. Put chicken in baking dish. Add flour and cinnamon to drippings in pan in which chicken was browned; mix thoroughly. Add chicken broth slowly, stirring over low heat until slightly thickened. Add chocolate, onion, carrots, and raisins. Pour over chicken. Cover chicken and bake 35 to 45 minutes or until chicken is tender. Garnish with almonds, if desired. SERVES 4–6.

"By the way, I hope you like Caesar salad," [Mountclemens said]. *It was a man's salad, zesty and full of crunch.*

Caesar Salad

———

3	tablespoons butter or margarine
2	slices bread, cut into ½-inch cubes
1	small clove garlic, minced
1	egg, at room temperature
1	clove garlic, cut in half
2	tablespoons salad oil
	Worcestershire sauce
2	tablespoons lemon juice
5	cups romaine lettuce, torn into pieces, washed and dried
¼	cup grated Parmesan cheese
	pepper to taste
1	2-ounce can anchovy fillets

Heat butter or margarine in skillet. Add bread cubes and minced garlic. Fry until the bread is crisp and golden. Remove from pan. Put croutons aside for later use. Next, coddle egg by putting egg into a pan of boiling water while still in shell. Immediately remove pan from heat and let it stand 1 minute. Rub salad bowl with cut garlic. Then add salad oil, a few dashes of Worcestershire sauce, and lemon juice to bowl. Break egg into bowl and beat with fork until well-mixed with other ingredients. Add lettuce and toss gently. Sprinkle with croutons, Parmesan cheese, and pepper. Top with anchovy fillets. SERVES 4–6.

Then came a **bittersweet chocolate dessert** with a velvet texture, and Qwilleran felt miraculously in harmony with a world in which art critics could cook like French chefs and cats could read . . . Later they had small cups of Turkish coffee in the living room, and Mountclemens said, "How are you enjoying your new milieu?"

Chocolate Mousse

¼ cup + 2 tablespoons sugar
¼ cup water
3 squares bittersweet chocolate, chopped
2 egg yolks, beaten until thick and lemon-colored
2 egg whites, pasteurized
¾ cup whipping cream

Place all but 2 tablespoons of the sugar, water, and chocolate into a small saucepan. Cook over low heat, stirring until sugar dissolves and chocolate melts. Stir the chocolate mixture slowly into the egg yolks. Put this mixture back into the pan and cook over low heat, stirring, for 1 minute. Remove from heat and cool. Beat egg whites until soft peaks form. Add the 2 tablespoons of sugar gradually and beat until stiff peaks form. Blend the chocolate mixture into the egg whites. Beat the whipping cream and fold it into the chocolate–egg white mixture. Pour into individual serving dishes and chill. SERVES 4.

À La Carte

Wednesday morning Qwilleran went upstairs with the plane ticket and knocked on Mountclemens's door.

"Good morning, Mr. Qwilleran . . . I hope you're not in a hurry. I have a ramekin of **eggs with herbs and sour cream**, ready to put in the oven, if you can wait. And some **chicken livers and bacon en brochette**."

"For that I can wait," said Qwilleran.

Herbed Eggs with Sour Cream

6 large eggs
6 tablespoons sour cream
1 tablespoon all-purpose flour
¼ teaspoon salt
⅛ teaspoon pepper
½ teaspoon chopped fresh chives
sour cream and chives for garnish (optional)

Preheat oven to 400°. Whisk eggs in mixing bowl. Add sour cream, flour, salt, pepper, and chives. Whisk briskly. Pour into 1-quart buttered baking ramekin. Bake 15 to 18 minutes or until eggs reach preferred degree of doneness. Garnish with dollop of sour cream and extra sprinkle of chives, if desired. SERVES 2–4.

*"The table is set in the kitchen, and we can have a **compote of fresh pineapple** while we keep an eye on the broiler . . . I dry my own herbs,"* Mountclemens explained. *"Do you appreciate a little mint marinated with the pineapple? I think it gives the fruit another dimension. Pineapple can be a little too direct."*

Pineapple Compote

1 fresh pineapple (about 4 cups)
2 teaspoons dried mint
1 tablespoon brown sugar

Peel and core pineapple. (Most grocery stores will peel and core pineapples if requested.) Discard core along with peelings. Cut the rest of the pineapple into bite-sized pieces. Stir brown sugar and mint into pineapple. Marinate for 30 minutes before serving. SERVES 4–6

*Qwilleran had just experienced the first forkful of **chicken livers rolled in bacon** and seasoned with a touch of basil, and he rolled his eyes gratefully heavenward.*

Chicken Livers and Bacon en Brochette

½ pound chicken livers
10 slices bacon

1 teaspoon dried basil
pepper to taste
toothpicks, soaked in water
small skewers (optional)

Preheat oven to 400°. Cut chicken livers and bacon slices into halves. Wrap a half slice of bacon around each chicken liver half. If livers are small you may wish to cut the bacon into thirds. Secure bacon with toothpicks. After bacon is wrapped around livers, they may be left as individual servings or multiple liver pieces can be placed on small skewers. Season with basil and pepper. Bake, uncovered, on a rack in a broiler pan about 30 minutes or until bacon is crisp. SERVES 4–6.

"Oh, there you are!" said the critic [Mountclemens] *amiably. "I had just come downstairs to invite you for a cup of Lapsang Souchong and some dessert. Rather laboriously I transported home a Dobos torte from a very fine Viennese bakery in New York."* . . .

Qwilleran let rich buttery chocolate melt slowly on his tongue.

Dobos Torte

6 eggs, separated
1½ cups sugar
1½ cups all-purpose flour
½ teaspoon salt
1 teaspoon baking powder
⅓ cup cold water
2 teaspoons vanilla extract
½ teaspoon cream of tartar

Preheat oven to 325°. Lightly grease and flour 4 eight-inch round cake pans. If you don't have 4 pans, use 2 and refrigerate the rest of the batter until the first 2 are baked. Beat egg yolks until thick—about 5 or 6 minutes. Slowly add sugar. Then sift or mix the flour, salt, and baking powder and add it to the egg mixture, alternating with a mixture of the water and vanilla extract. Beat egg whites and cream of tartar until stiff. Fold egg whites into the batter. Divide the batter evenly among the pans. Bake 30 minutes or until tops spring back when touched lightly in center. Cool layers about 5 minutes. Then loosen edges of the layers and invert them on wire racks until completely cool. Use a long knife or a piece of sewing thread to split the 4 layers into 8 layers. Frost between each layer as well as on the sides with chocolate frosting. Put caramel topping on top layer. Topping will be very brittle when cool. SERVES 10–12.

Chocolate frosting:

- 10 ounces melted unsweetened chocolate (cooled)
- 1 cup butter or margarine, room temperature
- 10 cups powdered sugar
- 10 tablespoons cold coffee or water

Mix the melted, cooled chocolate and butter or margarine. Beat in powdered sugar and half the coffee or water. Add additional coffee or water until frosting is of consistency to be easily spread.

Caramel topping:

Place 1 cup of granulated sugar into a skillet. Stirring constantly over low heat, cook until the sugar is melted and golden brown. Be careful not to scorch it. Pour and spread melted sugar over the top of the cake. Topping will harden immediately, hence the name *Dobos* or *Drum Torte*.

Qwilleran went to dinner at the Artist and Model, a snug cellar hideaway favored by the culture crowd. The background music was classical, the menu was French, and the walls were hung with works of art. They were totally unviewable in the cultivated gloom of the basement, and even the food—small portions served on brown earthenware—was difficult for the fork to find.

He ordered *ragôut de boeuf Bordelaise.*

Ragôut de Boeuf Bordelaise

¼ cup oil
¼ cup butter or margarine
2½ pounds round or chuck steak, cut into 2-inch cubes
salt and pepper to taste
2 onions, chopped
2 carrots, chopped
2 stalks celery, chopped
2 cloves garlic, minced
½ cup all-purpose flour
2 10½-ounce cans beef broth
1 cup dry red wine
2 14½-ounce cans diced tomatoes
2 bay leaves
¼ teaspoon dried thyme
10 pearl onions
5 carrots, halved
10 small potatoes, peeled
1 tablespoon chopped fresh parsley

Heat the oil and butter or margarine in stockpot and brown the meat over high heat. Season with salt and pepper. Add the chopped onion, chopped carrot, celery, and garlic. Reduce heat and cook until onion is lightly browned. Add the flour; stir and cook until flour is blended into mixture. Add beef broth and wine and bring to boil. Add tomatoes, bay leaves, and thyme. Cover and cook over low heat 1½ hours or until meat is nearly tender. Add pearl onions, halved carrots, and potatoes. Cover and cook 1 hour. Season with additional salt and pepper, if desired. Remove bay leaves before serving. Sprinkle with parsley. SERVES 8–10.

The Cat Who Ate Danish Modern

Qwilleran never imagined in his wildest dreams he would be covering the interior design beat. But that's exactly what he's doing. When a woman is found murdered, he and Koko start sifting clues. Enter Yum Yum, who both Qwilleran and Koko agree is the best thing that has happened to them in a long time.

Villa Verandah
Buffet

Royal Caviar

Shrimp Kabobs

Welsh Rarebit

Marinated Mushrooms

Stuffed Artichoke Hearts

Savory Meatballs in Dill Sauce

🐾

"Why don't you come to my apartment for cocktails this evening? [asked David Lyke] I'll have a few decorators on tap."

"Good idea! [said Qwilleran] Where do you live?"

"At the Villa Verandah. That's the new apartment house that looks like a bent waffle." . . .

It was not the bar that interested Qwilleran. It was the buffet. It was laden with caviar, shrimp, a rarebit in a chafing dish, marinated mushrooms, stuffed artichoke hearts, and savory meatballs in a dill sauce.

Royal Caviar

6 ounces red caviar, any variety
6 ounces black caviar, any variety
2 8-ounce packages cream cheese, room temperature
2 tablespoons lemon juice
3 tablespoons chopped green onion
1 teaspoon Worcestershire sauce
¼ cup sliced green olives
2 tablespoons dried parsley
assorted crackers or toast points

Rinse and drain caviars. Cream the cheese with the lemon juice, green onion, and Worcestershire sauce. Shape cheese mixture into a circle approximately 8 inches in diameter and 1 inch thick. Cover a 5-inch circle in the center of the cheese mixture with the red caviar. Ring the outside of the caviar with sliced olives. Beside the olives make a ring of black caviar, covering the rest of the top of the cheese circle. Press the parsley into the sides of the circle. Place any remaining black caviar around the outside of the circle. Serve with toast points or crackers. SERVES 12.

Shrimp Kabobs

⅛ cup cider vinegar
¼ cup vegetable oil
1 clove garlic, chopped
¼ teaspoon dried dill weed
¼ teaspoon dried parsley
½ teaspoon salt
¼ teaspoon pepper
6 asparagus stalks
1 pound large fresh shrimp (about 24)
sturdy party toothpicks

Mix vinegar, oil, garlic, dill weed, parsley, salt, and pepper. Cut each asparagus stalk into 4 pieces. Skewer the shrimp and asparagus pieces on toothpicks and put them in the marinade, turning to coat. Cover and refrigerate for 2–3 hours. Drain the kabobs, discarding marinade, and broil them about 2–3 minutes on each side approximately 4 inches from the heat. SERVES 12.

Welsh Rarebit

¼ cup butter or margarine
2 tablespoons all-purpose flour
½ teaspoon dry mustard
1 teaspoon Worcestershire sauce
¾ cup half-and-half
¾ cup beer
1½ cups shredded cheddar cheese
salt to taste
dash of red pepper
6 slices toast or 3 English muffins, split

Melt butter or margarine in a saucepan. Add the flour, mustard, and Worcestershire sauce. Stir constantly over medium heat until smooth. Slowly stir in the half-and-half and the beer. Reduce heat to low, add the cheese, stirring until cheese melts. Season with salt and pepper. Spoon over toast or muffins. SERVES 4.

Marinated Mushrooms

¼ cup lemon juice
¼ cup salad oil
¼ cup finely chopped onion
1 clove garlic, minced
1 tablespoon finely chopped fresh parsley or 1 teaspoon dried parsley
¾ teaspoon salt
¼ teaspoon black pepper
¼ teaspoon sugar
3 cups sliced fresh mushrooms or small mushroom caps

Mix the lemon juice, salad oil, onion, garlic, parsley, salt, pepper, and sugar. Put the mushrooms in a bowl and pour the dressing over them. Cover and refrigerate 3 hours to overnight, stirring several times. SERVES 4–6.

Stuffed Artichoke Hearts

¼ cup + 2 tablespoons butter
¼ cup all-purpose flour
2 cups half-and-half
¼ teaspoon salt
⅛ teaspoon pepper
2 cups shredded, cooked chicken
6 artichoke hearts or bottoms, cooked
Parmesan cheese, grated

Preheat oven to 375°. Melt ¼ cup butter in a saucepan and add flour. Add the half-and-half, stirring until thickened—about 3 minutes. Add salt and pepper. Mix half the sauce with the chicken. Stuff the artichokes with the chicken mixture. Arrange in a baking dish. Cover with the remaining sauce. Sprinkle with cheese and dot with remaining 2 tablespoons butter. Bake until sauce begins to bubble. SERVES 6.

Savory Meatballs in Dill Sauce

1 pound lean ground beef
¼ cup rolled oats or bread crumbs
5 slices bacon, cooked and crumbled fine
⅓ cup milk
1 egg, beaten
¼ teaspoon pepper
¼ teaspoon savory
¼ teaspoon + ¼ teaspoon dried dill weed
1 14½-ounce can beef broth
2 tablespoons cornstarch

Combine ground beef, rolled oats or bread crumbs, bacon, milk, egg, pepper, savory, and ¼ teaspoon dill weed. Form into small meatballs and place in a saucepan. Pour the beef broth, reserving 2 tablespoonsful over the meatballs. Bring to a boil over medium heat. Reduce heat to low; cover and cook 15–20 minutes. Remove meatballs from pan with slotted spoon. Add the 2 tablespoons reserved beef broth to cornstarch and blend. Put cornstarch and broth mixture into broth in the saucepan from which meatballs were taken. Add ¼ teaspoon dill weed and cook until thickened. Return meatballs to saucepan and simmer 5 minutes. SERVES 6.

À La Carte

"Have a cocktail?" Qwilleran invited. "I'm on the wagon myself, but I'll have a lemon and seltzer to keep you company."

*". . . I'll make us one of **nature's own cocktails** if you'll order the ingredients and two champagne glasses." [said Cokey]*

Nature's Own Cocktail

3   tablespoons cream
cold ginger ale
pinch of freshly gound nutmeg

Pour cream into 8-ounce glass. Fill glass with ginger ale. Stir just enough to incorporate cream into ginger ale. Dust surface with nutmeg.

*She [Cokey] looked at the menu and asked for **brook trout** with a large garnish of parsley, and a **small salad**. Qwilleran compared her taut figure with his own well-padded beltline and felt guilty as he ordered **bean soup**, a hefty steak, and a baked potato with sour cream.*

Brook Trout

2	quarts water
3	large stalks celery, chopped
1	carrot, sliced thin
5	sprigs parsley, shredded
3	bay leaves
4	whole cloves
3	slices lemon
2	teaspoons vinegar
2	teaspoons salt
6	8-ounce trout, cleaned

Place water in large saucepan. Add celery, carrots, parsley, bay leaves, cloves, lemon slices, vinegar, and salt. Bring to a boil. Simmer for 10 to 15 minutes. Cut trout into serving pieces. Add to saucepan with vegetables. Simmer until tender. Remove trout; discard vegetables. Garnish with additional parsley when served, if desired. SERVES 6–8.

Salad with Poppy Seed Dressing

1	small onion, chopped
1½	cups sugar

⅔   cup cider vinegar
2   teaspoons dry mustard
1½   teaspoons salt
2   cups vegetable oil
2   tablespoons poppy seeds
salad greens

Place onion, sugar, vinegar, mustard, and salt in a blender. Blend well. With blender still running, add oil in a thin stream. Continue to blend until thick and creamy. Add poppy seeds. Blend 5–10 seconds. Wash and dry salad greens. Serve with Poppy Seed dressing. MAKES APPROXIMATELY 3½ CUPS DRESSING.

Bean Soup

2   cups dried great northern beans
1   ham bone or 1 pound ham butt, cut into small pieces
6   cups water
½   cup chopped onion
1   medium carrot, chopped
1   stalk celery, chopped
salt and pepper to taste
1   tablespoon all-purpose flour (optional)
½   cup water (optional)

Soak beans according to package directions. Drain. Place beans, ham, and 6 cups water in a large saucepan. Cook 2½ hours over low heat. If ham bone was used, remove at this point. Add onion, carrot, celery, salt, and pepper. Cook until vegetables are tender. For thicker broth, combine the flour and water and add to the mixture. Cook 10 minutes longer. SERVES 6–8.

The Cat Who Turned On and Off

Qwilleran is looking for something different on which to do a feature series. Junktown, with its antique dealers and collectors, promises a colorful story. But when one of Junktown's citizens falls and is killed, Qwilleran and Koko are out to prove it was murder.

Mrs. Cobb's
Junktown Dinner

Cranberry Juice Cocktail

Piroshki

Pot Roast

Mashed Potatoes

Salad with Roquefort Dressing

Mrs. Cobb's Coconut Cake

🐾

"Why don't you have dinner with us around seven o'clock, and then you won't have to go out of the house . . . We're having pot roast *and* mashed potatoes—*nothing fancy. Just* potatoes whipped with sour cream and dill. *And a* salad with Roquefort dressing. *And* coconut cake *for dessert."* [Invitation to Qwilleran from Iris Cobb]

  "I'll be there," said Qwilleran.

Mrs. Cobb, playing the fussy hostess . . . served small glasses of cranberry juice cocktail *on plates with lace paper doilies.*

Cranberry Juice Cocktail

6   cups cranberry juice
2   tablespoons lemon juice
1   cup apple juice
1   cup orange juice
extra-fine sugar or honey to taste

Mix ingredients. Serve chilled. SERVES 4–6.

[Mrs. Cobb] *passed a platter of tiny meat turnovers . . . C.C. said, "Who you trying to impress with this fancy grub?"*

"Our new tenant, of course. I wouldn't slave over piroshki *for a slob like you," she said sweetly.*

Piroshki

Filling:
- ¼ pound ground beef
- ½ cup finely chopped onion
- 1 teaspoon dried dill weed
- ½ teaspoon salt
- ⅛ teaspoon pepper
- 1 hard-boiled egg, finely chopped
- 1 egg yolk
- 1 tablespoon cold water

Preheat oven to 375°. Place the ground beef, onion, dill weed, salt, and pepper into a skillet. Cook over very low heat, stirring frequently, crushing any large lumps of ground beef to make a very fine filling. Drain fat and add hard-boiled egg. While filling is cooling, make the pastry. Roll one ball out on a floured surface to ⅛ inch thickness and cut with a glass or biscuit cutter into 2½–3 inch circles. Place filling on bottom half of pastry by rounded ½ teaspoonful. Moisten the top edge and fold down over the filling. Press edges with fingers. Edges can be pressed with fork tines if they don't hold together. Repeat with remaining dough. Mix egg yolk and water. Gently brush pastries with egg yolk mixture. Bake about 15 minutes on ungreased cookie sheets, or until pastry is golden brown. MAKES ABOUT 4 DOZEN.

Pastry:
- ½   cup butter, softened
- 2   cups self-rising flour
- ½   cup sour cream
- 1   egg

Cut the butter into the flour until the mixture is about the size of peas. Add the sour cream and egg. Mix well. Form into 2 balls for easier handling.

*When seven o'clock arrived, whiffs of **beef simmering with garlic and celery tops** beckoned the newsman across the hall to the Cobbs' apartment.*

Pot Roast

- 3–4   pounds of round bottom or rump roast
- oil (optional)
- garlic salt
- pepper
- 1   large onion
- several celery tops
- water

Preheat oven to 325°. Meat can be browned on both sides in oil, if desired. Then place in a roasting pan or heavy glass baking dish. Sprinkle meat with garlic salt and pepper. Slice onion and place on top of roast along with celery tops. Add about an inch and a half of water to the pan. Cover tightly. Bake until fork-tender, about 4 hours. SERVES 6.

Mashed Potatoes

7 medium potatoes
2 tablespoons butter or margarine, room temperature
½ cup warm milk (approximate)
½ cup sour cream, room temperature
½ teaspoon dried dill weed
salt and pepper to taste

Peel and slice or dice potatoes. Boil until tender. Drain, mash with potato masher or electric mixer. (Mrs. Cobb always leaves a few lumps so they'll taste like the "*real thing*.") Blend in butter or margarine, milk, sour cream, dill weed, salt, and pepper. SERVES 4–6.

Salad with Roquefort Dressing

4 ounces crumbled Roquefort cheese
1 cup sour cream
1½ teaspoons lemon juice
¼ cup buttermilk
1 teaspoon finely chopped white onion
salt and pepper to taste
lettuce of choice

Mix all ingredients except lettuce together. Refrigerate several hours or overnight before serving. Wash, dry, and tear lettuce into bite-sized pieces. Serve with Roquefort dressing. MAKES APPROXIMATELY 1½ CUPS DRESSING.

Mrs. Cobb's Coconut Cake

Cake:

1½	cups sugar
½	cup shortening
2	cups all-purpose flour
3	teaspoons baking powder
¾	teaspoon salt
1	cup milk
5	egg whites
1	teaspoon almond extract
1	cup flaked coconut

Preheat oven to 350°. Using an electric mixer, cream the sugar and shortening until light and fluffy. Sift or mix the flour, baking powder, and salt. While beating, add the flour mixture to the creamed sugar and shortening, alternating with the milk. Then beat for 2 to 2½ minutes at medium speed. Add the egg whites and almond extract. Beat another 1½ minutes. Add the coconut and stir well. Put into two greased and floured 9-inch cake pans. Bake about 30 minutes or until toothpick inserted in center comes out clean. Cool 10 minutes before removing layers from pans. Spread apricot filling on completely cooled bottom layer. Place second layer over filling. Cover top and sides of both layers with frosting. SERVES 10–12.

Filling:

1	15-ounce can apricots
2	tablespoons cornstarch
2	tablespoons sugar

Drain apricots, reserving 2 tablespoons of the juice. Remove any pit fragments or pieces of stems from the apricots. Puree in blender until smooth. Place in saucepan. Add reserved juice to cornstarch and mix well. Stir into apricots. Add the sugar. Cook, stirring, over medium heat until thickened.

Frosting:

- 6 tablespoons butter or margarine, room temperature
- 6 ounces cream cheese, room temperature
- 3 cups powdered sugar
- ½ teaspoon vanilla extract
- milk, as needed
- extra coconut (optional)

Cream the butter or margarine and cream cheese together. Add powdered sugar and vanilla extract. If frosting is too stiff to spread, add milk a half-teaspoonful at a time. After cake is frosted, lightly press more coconut onto the top and sides, if desired.

À La Carte

Soon Qwilleran was sitting in a gilded chair at the lopsided table, plunging a fork into bubbling hot pie with sharp cheese melted over the top. Mrs. Cobb watched with pleasure as her prospective tenant devoured every crumb of flaky crust and every dribble of spiced juice. "Have some more?" [she asked]

"I shouldn't." Qwilleran pulled in his waistline. "But it's very good."

"Oh, come on! You don't have to worry about weight. You have a very nice physique."

The newsman tackled his second wedge of pie, and Mrs. Cobb described the joys of living in an old house.

Mrs. Cobb's Apple Pie with Cheese

Pastry:

- 2 cups all-purpose flour
- 1 teaspoon salt
- ⅔ cup shortening
- 5–6 tablespoons ice water

Mix flour and salt. Cut in shortening until mixture is about the size of peas. Add water a table-spoonful at a time, mixing lightly with fork. When dough holds together, form into loose ball; divide in half. Roll 1 ball out to ¼ inch in thickness on floured surface. Place in 9-inch pie pan. Roll out second portion of dough to ¼ inch in thickness; reserve for top crust.

Filling:

- ¾ cup brown sugar, firmly packed
- ¾ cup granulated sugar
- 2 tablespoons all-purpose flour
- ¾ teaspoon cinnamon
- ⅛ teaspoon nutmeg
- ¼ teaspoon salt
- 8 cups apples, peeled, sliced
- 2 tablespoons butter or margarine
- cheddar cheese slices

Preheat oven to 425°. Combine sugars, flour, cinnamon, nutmeg, and salt. Stir dry ingredients into the sliced apples. Place into pastry-lined 9-inch pie pan. Cut the butter or margarine into small pieces and spread them on top of the apples. Add top crust. Pinch the edges together. Make slits in top so steam can escape. Bake 1 hour or until crust is golden brown and apples are tender. Before serving, place a slice of cheddar cheese on the top of each piece of pie. Place under the broiler and heat until cheese melts. SERVES 6.

"And why don't you let me fix you a bite of breakfast? [asked Iris Cobb] I made corn muffins for C.C. before he went picketing, and there's half a panful left."

Qwilleran remembered the sticky breakfast roll glued to its limp paper wrapper—and accepted. Later, while he was eating bacon and eggs and buttering hot **corn muffins**, *Iris talked to him of the antiques business.*

Corn Muffins

2 eggs
2 tablespoons oil or melted butter or margarine
1 cup water
½ cup buttermilk
2 cups corn meal
2 teaspoons baking powder
1 teaspoon salt
1 tablespoon sugar

Preheat oven to 450°. Place a muffin pan or 9-inch round pan generously greased with shortening in the oven to heat. Beat eggs in mixing bowl. Add the oil or butter or margarine, water, buttermilk, corn meal, baking powder, salt, and sugar. Stir until well-blended. Pour batter into the hot pan and bake 20 minutes or until golden brown. Makes 8 large muffins or one 9-inch pan of cornbread. Serve with butter. SERVES 6–8.

It was then that he spotted the shop of The Three Weird Sisters, its window filled with washbowl and pitcher sets, spittoons, and the inevitable spinning wheel . . . Three women wearing orange smocks stopped what they were doing and turned to regard the man with a bushy moustache. Qwilleran returned their gaze. For a moment he was speechless . . . Flashing her dimples, the brunette said to Qwilleran, "Would you have a bowl of chowder with us? And some cheese and crackers?" If they had offered hardtack and goose grease, he would have accepted.

Clam Chowder

2 slices bacon, cut into small pieces
1 stalk celery, chopped
1 medium onion, chopped
2 medium potatoes, peeled and diced
1 tablespoon butter
2 tablespoons all-purpose flour
1 8-ounce bottle or can clam juice
salt and pepper to taste
2 6½-ounce cans minced or chopped clams, drained; reserve liquid
1½ quarts half-and-half
¼ teaspoon dried thyme
2 teaspoons chopped fresh parsley

Fry the bacon until partially cooked. Add the celery and onion. Sauté until the vegetables are tender and the bacon is crisp. Add the potatoes and butter. Sprinkle the flour over the potatoes and mix well. Stir in the reserved liquid, clam juice, salt, and pepper. Cook over low heat until the potatoes are tender, stirring occasionally. Add the clams. Then stir in the half-and-half, thyme, and parsley. Heat until hot, but do not boil. SERVES 6.

In the afternoon Qwilleran spent a satisfactory hour with the managing editor, and then joined the Women's Department for **pink lemonade** *and* **Christmas cookies,** *and later turned up at an impromptu celebration in the Photo Lab, where he was the only sober guest, and eventually went home.*

Festive Pink Lemonade

8 cups water
2 cups sugar
¾ cup lemon juice
¼ cup maraschino cherry juice

Bring 2 cups of the water to a boil. Add the sugar to the water. Stir over medium heat until sugar is dissolved. Add the lemon and maraschino cherry juice to the sugar-water. Pour juice mixture and the remaining water into a pitcher. Stir and chill. SERVES 10–12.

Pineapple Cookies

1 cup shortening
½ cup sugar
1 egg
1 8-ounce can crushed pineapple with juice

3½   cups all-purpose flour
1   teaspoon baking soda
1   teaspoon salt
¼   teaspoon nutmeg
½   cup chopped pecans or walnuts

Preheat oven to 400°. Cream shortening and sugar until light and fluffy. Add the egg. Stir in crushed pineapple with juice. Sift or mix flour, baking soda, salt, and nutmeg. Stir dry ingredients into the pineapple mixture. Mix in nuts. Chill 1 hour. Drop by teaspoonsful 2 inches apart on lightly greased baking sheet. Bake 8–10 minutes. MAKES ABOUT 5 DOZEN.

Plum Pecan Cookies

¼   cup shortening
¼   cup butter or margarine
¼   cup brown sugar
1   egg, separated
½   teaspoon vanilla extract
1   cup all-purpose flour
¼   teaspoon salt
½   cup chopped pecans
plum jelly

Preheat oven to 375°. Cream shortening, butter or margarine, and brown sugar. Add the egg yolk and vanilla extract. Then add flour and salt. Beat egg white slightly. Shape the dough into 1-inch balls. Roll balls in the egg white and then in the chopped nuts. Place on ungreased cookie sheet about 1 inch apart. Make an indentation in the center of each with a spoon. Bake 10–12 minutes. When cool, fill the centers with plum jelly. MAKES ABOUT 2 DOZEN.

Christmas Kringler

Preheat oven to 350°.

Crust:

1 stick butter or margarine
1 cup all-purpose flour
1 tablespoon water

Cut butter or margarine into flour; moisten with water. Form into a ball and pat onto ungreased cookie sheet in two 3-inch by 12-inch strips.

Filling:

1 cup water
1 stick butter or margarine
1 cup all-purpose flour
3 eggs
1 teaspoon almond or vanilla extract

Place water and butter or margarine in saucepan. Bring to a boil. Remove from heat; add flour, stirring until smooth. Beat in eggs, 1 at a time. Stir in extract. Continue stirring until filling leaves sides of pan and forms ball. Spread on unbaked crusts. Bake for 55–60 minutes or until lightly browned. Cool, frost the strips of pastry with icing, and decorate. Cut into 1 inch bars. MAKES 24 BARS.

Icing:

2 cups confectioners' sugar
2 tablespoons half-and-half
2 tablespoons butter or margarine, softened
1 teaspoon almond extract or ½ teaspoon vanilla extract

Mix sugar, half-and-half, butter or margarine, and extract. Add more half-and-half, if necessary, to make spreading easy.

Decorations

maraschino cherries, red and green
pecans, chopped

"Koko, you're a hero!" Mary said to the cat, who was now taking his lordly ease on the daybed. "And you're going to have a reward. Pressed duck!" She turned to Qwilleran. "I took the liberty of ordering dinner. It's being sent over from the Toledo Restaurant. I hope you like oysters Rockefeller and pressed duck and chateaubriand and French strawberries."

Oysters Rockefeller

2   cups chopped fresh spinach
3   tablespoons chopped onion
1   tablespoon chopped celery
2   tablespoons chopped fresh parsley
1   clove garlic, minced
4   tablespoons + 1 tablespoon butter or margarine
several drops of hot sauce
¼   teaspoon salt
½   cup fine dry bread crumbs
½   tablespoon water
aluminum foil
24   oysters on the half shell

Preheat oven to 425°. Cook the spinach in boiling water until tender. Drain and squeeze out water. Sauté the onion, celery, parsley, and garlic in 4 tablespoons of the butter or margarine. Put the spinach, sautéed vegetables, hot sauce, salt, and ¼ cup of bread crumbs into a food processor and process until smooth. If necessary, add the water to make the mixture more moist. Crumple aluminum foil and place it on the bottom of a baking pan or cookie sheet. Place the oyster shells on the foil to keep them from tipping. Place a rounded teaspoonful of the spinach mixture on each oyster. Mix the remaining bread crumbs and butter together and place on top of the spinach mixture. Bake about 10 minutes or until the oysters are plump and the edges begin to curl. Broil, if desired, to brown tops. SERVES 6.

French Strawberries

———————

4   cups halved strawberries
3   tablespoons orange juice concentrate or orange-flavored liqueur
½   cup + 2 tablespoons powdered sugar
½   pint whipping cream
2   tablespoons sour cream
⅛   teaspoon vanilla extract
⅛–¼   teaspoon cinnamon

Sprinkle strawberries with orange concentrate or liqueur and ½ cup sugar; stir. Refrigerate about 90 minutes. Whip cream until soft peaks form. Stir in 2 tablespoons sugar, sour cream, vanilla extract, and cinnamon. Fold chilled strawberries into whipped cream mixture. SERVES 4–6.

The Cat Who Saw Red

*E*veryone knows how hard it is to go on a diet. Now Qwilleran is faced with the prospect of trying to diet while working on his new assignment—writing a regular column on the enjoyment of good food and wine. Then he and his felines move into the Maus Haus and right into the middle of a mystery.

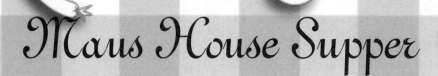

Maus House Supper

Broiled Oysters

Maus's Cream of Watercress Soup

Jellied Clams

Stuffed Breast of Chicken

Braised Endive

Curried Tomatoes

Romaine Salad

Crêpes Suzette

🐾

He took a taxi to the River Road residence of Robert Maus . . .

The two women [Hixie Rice and Rosemary Whiting] were standing near a sideboard that held platters of hors d'oeuvres. She [Hixie] stopped to pop a bacon-wrapped oyster into her mouth.

Broiled Oysters

18   large oysters, fresh, canned, or frozen
garlic powder
salt and pepper
paprika
12   slices bacon, cut into thirds
36   sturdy party toothpicks

Cut oysters in half. Sprinkle with garlic powder, salt, pepper, and paprika. Wrap a piece of bacon around each oyster half. Secure with a toothpick. Broil 10 minutes or until bacon is crisp. Turn over and broil an additional 5 minutes until bacon crisps on other side. (Toothpicks can be soaked in water so they won't burn.) MAKES 36 HORS D'OEUVRES.

"What's on the menu tonight, Willie?" [asked Hixie]

"Not much. Just cream of watercress soup, jellied clams, stuffed breast of chicken baked in a crust, braised endive—I hate endive—broiled curried tomatoes, romaine salad, and crepes suzette."

*The table was laid with heavy ceramic plates and pewter serving pieces on the bare oak boards, and it was lighted by candles in massive wrought-iron candelabra . . . Spoons were raised. Qwilleran tasted the **watercress soup** and found it delicately delicious, yet he had no overwhelming desire to finish it. A sense of elation had banished his appetite.*

Maus's Cream of Watercress Soup

2 cups chopped fresh watercress
1 small onion, finely chopped
3 tablespoons butter or margarine
3 cups light cream
2 10¾–ounce cans cream of chicken soup
salt and pepper to taste
¼ cup white wine (optional)

Sauté the chopped watercress and onions in the butter or margarine. In a saucepan, mix cream and cream of chicken soup, stirring until smooth. Heat, but do not boil. Add watercress and onions to the cream and soup mixture. Simmer about 5 minutes. Add salt and pepper. Remove from heat and add wine, if desired. SERVES 6.

William removed the soup bowls from the right, served the clams from the left, and poured a white wine, while whistling a tune off-key.

Jellied Clams

---

1 envelope unflavored gelatin
1 14½-ounce can chicken broth plus clam juice to make 2 cups liquid total
1 6½-ounce can minced clams, drained with liquid reserved
1 teaspoon lemon juice
½ teaspoon Worcestershire sauce
2 hard-boiled eggs, thinly sliced
12 sliced stuffed olives
lettuce leaves

Soak the gelatin in ¼ cup of the broth and clam juice. Add the lemon juice and Worcestershire sauce to the remaining broth. Heat 1 cup of this remaining broth almost to the boiling point. Put the soaked gelatin into it. Then return the dissolved gelatin to the rest of the liquid; stir well. Add the clams. Pour into lightly buttered ½-cup molds. Add slices of eggs and olives. Refrigerate until set. Turn out on lettuce leaves. SERVES 6.

The chicken was served, and again Qwilleran found it easy to abstain.
He toyed with his food and listened to the voices around him.

Stuffed Breast of Chicken

4 skinless chicken breasts
½ teaspoon salt
¼ teaspoon pepper
2 tablespoons + 2 tablespoons butter or margarine
½ cup chopped onion
½ cup chopped mushrooms, fresh or canned
¼ cup chopped celery
½ cup finely chopped carrots
¼ teaspoon minced fresh garlic
2 phyllo dough sheets

Preheat oven to 350°. Pound chicken breasts to flatten. Season with salt and pepper. In a skillet, melt 2 tablespoons butter or margarine. Add the onion, mushrooms, celery, carrots, and garlic. Sauté vegetables 5 minutes. Place 2–3 tablespoons of the vegetables on each breast. Roll the breasts, tucking in the sides to keep the vegetables secured. Then roll the breast in half a phyllo dough sheet. Place in a baking dish, folded side down. Melt remaining 2 tablespoons butter or margarine and brush on top of phyllo dough. Bake 45 minutes or until golden brown and tender. SERVES 4.

Braised Endive

3 cups chopped endive
¼ cup butter or margarine

salt and pepper to taste
½   teaspoon dried dill weed

Cook endive in ½ inch of salted water for 6 minutes or until tender. Drain. Then brown endive in the butter or margarine. Stir in additional salt, if desired, pepper, and dill weed before serving. SERVES 4.

Curried Tomatoes

4   medium-sized tomatoes
½   cup finely crushed bread crumbs
¼   cup Parmesan cheese
½   teaspoon curry powder
¼   teaspoon salt
¼   teaspoon pepper
4   teaspoons butter or margarine

Preheat oven to 375°. Wash the tomatoes, remove stems, and cut into halves horizontally. If necessary, cut a small section off the bottom of each portion so the tomato half will sit evenly. Mix the bread crumbs, Parmesan cheese, curry powder, salt, and pepper. Press the top of the tomato halves into the bread crumb mixture. Place ½ teaspoon butter or margarine on top of each tomato half. Bake on a greased cookie sheet until tender, approximately 20 minutes. Place under broiler until brown. SERVES 4.

His pronouncement had a dampening effect on the conversation. All heads immediately bent over salads. Suddenly everyone was intent on spearing romaine.

Romaine Salad

Dressing:

- ½ cup vegetable oil
- 6 tablespoons sugar
- 6 tablespoons white vinegar
- ½ teaspoon salt
- dash of pepper

Mix all ingredients. Heat until sugar dissolves. Chill before serving.

Salad:

- 6 cups bite-sized pieces romaine lettuce
- 1 cup thinly sliced celery
- 1 small red onion, sliced
- 2 11-ounce cans mandarin oranges, drained
- ¼ cup sliced almonds

Place lettuce on individual salad plates. Layer celery, onion, and orange sections over lettuce and sprinkle with almonds. Pour dressing over all. SERVES 6.

Crêpes Suzette

Crêpes:

- 2 tablespoons butter or margarine
- 1 cup all-purpose flour
- ¼ cup sugar
- ¼ teaspoon salt
- 3 eggs
- 1 cup milk
- oil or butter

Melt butter or margarine and set aside. Sift or mix flour, sugar, and salt together. In a medium-sized bowl, beat eggs until thick. Add melted butter and milk to eggs. Combine egg mixture and dry ingredients. Beat until smooth. Put approximately 1 teaspoon oil or butter into 7-inch skillet or crêpe pan. Heat over medium heat until bubbly. Pour 3 tablespoons batter into skillet. Immediately spread batter over skillet bottom by tilting it back and forth. Cook until top is dry and bottom is light brown. Fold crêpe in half, then in half again, forming a triangle with the brown side out. Set aside. Repeat with remaining batter. SERVES 4.

Orange sauce:

- ½ cup butter or margarine
- ½ cup sugar
- 2½ teaspoons finely grated orange peel
- ½ cup orange juice
- ¼ cup orange liqueur
- 1 orange, sliced
- ¼ cup brandy

Combine butter or margarine, sugar, orange peel, orange juice, and orange liqueur, in a skillet. Cook, stirring constantly, until thickened. Put the crêpes in the sauce. Arrange the orange slices on top as decoration. Simmer for 5 minutes. In another small pan heat the brandy to simmering. Pour over the crêpes and ignite.

À La Carte

The meal was served at a big round table in a corner of the kitchen, because there were only six sitting down to dinner. . . . The room was heady with aromas: roast beef, cheese, logs burning in the fireplace, and Joy's spicy perfume . . . Qwilleran merely sampled the  *corn chowder . . .*

Corn Chowder

6 potatoes, peeled and diced
4 cups water
½ pound bacon, fried and crumbled
2 cups frozen whole kernel corn
1 teaspoon salt
¼ teaspoon pepper
1½ cups light cream

Place potatoes in a saucepan with water. Boil until tender. Add bacon, corn, salt, and pepper. Bring to a boil. Reduce heat to low. Simmer uncovered for 15 minutes. Stir in cream. Heat, but do not boil. SERVES 6.

. . . and [he] ate half of his portion of . . . broccoli parmigiana.

Broccoli Parmigiana

3   cups frozen chopped broccoli
½   teaspoon salt
1   small onion, grated
1   10¾-ounce can cream of chicken soup
½   cup mayonnaise
½   cup Parmesan cheese
1   teaspoon salt
¼   teaspoon pepper
6   eggs, beaten

Preheat oven to 300°. Put broccoli and salt in a saucepan with enough water to cover the broccoli. Cook until tender. Drain broccoli. In a bowl, mix the onion, soup, mayonnaise, cheese, salt, and pepper. Stir in the beaten eggs and fold into the broccoli. Pour into a greased casserole dish. Bake 1 hour or until firm. SERVES 6–8.

. . . and ignored a glob of mush flecked with green . . . Rosemary, the quiet one, glanced at the untouched glob on Qwilleran's salad plate. "You should eat the bulgur. *It's highly nutritious."*

Bulgur with Parsley

3 cups water
1 cup bulgur wheat
½ cup finely chopped celery
½ cup finely chopped onion
1 clove garlic, minced
1 tablespoon butter or margarine
4 teaspoons dried parsley
1 teaspoon salt
⅛ teaspoon pepper

Bring water to a boil in a saucepan. While stirring, slowly add the bulgur wheat. Reduce heat to low and simmer for 10 minutes. Remove from the heat and let sit, covered, for 20 minutes. Sauté the celery, onion, and garlic in the butter or margarine. Drain the bulgur, add the sautéed vegetables, parsley, salt, and pepper. SERVES 4.

Parker House Rolls

1 cup milk, scalded
1 package dry yeast
⅓ cup sugar
4 cups all-purpose flour
1 teaspoon salt

❧ *The Cat Who Saw Red* ❧

          2   eggs, beaten
      ⅓   cup butter or margarine, melted
      additional melted butter or margarine

Cool milk to lukewarm (105–115°). Put yeast and sugar into mixing bowl. Add the milk and stir. Add 2 cups of the flour, salt, eggs, and butter or margarine. Beat batter thoroughly. Add the rest of the flour gradually. Form into ball and place in greased bowl. Turn dough to grease the top. Cover and let rise, until doubled in size, approximately one hour. Roll dough on a floured surface to ½-inch in thickness. Cut into rounds using biscuit cutter or drinking glass. Make a crease just off-center with the dull side of a knife. Brush with melted butter or margarine. Fold the smaller side over the larger side. Place, crease-side down on buttered or greased baking sheet. Let rise again until double in size, approximately 45 minutes. Bake 15 to 20 minutes at 400°. MAKES ABOUT 2 DOZEN ROLLS.

"The big baby [Dan]!" his wife muttered. "I noticed he finished his **apple pie** *before he made his tempermental exit." . . . The meal ended with stilted scraps of conversation.*

Maus House Apple Pie

Pastry:
      2   cups all-purpose flour
      1   teaspoon salt
      ⅔   cup shortening
      5–6   tablespoons ice water

Mix flour and salt. Cut in shortening until mixture is about the size of peas. Add water a tablespoonful at a time, mixing lightly with fork. When dough holds together, form into loose ball; divide in half. Roll 1 portion of dough into a circle ¼-inch in thickness on floured surface. Place in 9-inch pie pan. Reserve second portion of dough for top crust.

Filling:

- 6 Mackintosh apples, peeled and sliced
- 1½ cups sugar
- 1 teaspoon cinnamon
- 1 teaspoon vanilla extract
- 2 teaspoons butter or margarine

Preheat oven to 400°. Mix apples, sugar, cinnamon, and vanilla extract. Place mixture in unbaked pastry-lined pie pan. Dot with butter or margarine. Roll out second portion of dough and place over apples. Crimp around edges. Make slits in crust to let steam escape. Bake about 60 minutes. SERVES 6.

When Qwilleran dressed and went downstairs, he followed the aroma of bacon and coffee into the kitchen. At the big round table Robert Maus was solemnly breakfasting on croissants and marmalade and French chocolate, while Hixie waited for Mrs. Marron to make French toast. Qwilleran helped himself to orange juice.

French Toast

½ cup milk

2 eggs, beaten

1 tablespoon sugar

1 teaspoon vanilla extract

dash of nutmeg

8 slices of French bread about 1-inch thick

3 tablespoons butter or margarine

maple syrup

chopped pecans

In a shallow dish stir together the milk, eggs, sugar, vanilla extract, and nutmeg. Soak bread slices about 2 minutes in the milk mixture. Turn the bread over to coat both sides. While bread is soaking, melt the butter or margarine in a skillet or on a griddle. Fry the bread until golden brown. Top with maple syrup and sprinkle with pecans. SERVES 4–6.

"Where are you eating tonight?" Riker asked.

"I've invited Maus to go with me to the Toledo Tombs," [answered Qwilleran] . . .

The two men were conducted to a table resplendent with white napery. Seven wineglasses and fourteen pieces of flat silver glittered at each place. Two waiters draped napkins, lightly scented with orange flower water, across the guests' knees. A captain presented menus bound in gold-tooled Florentine leather, and three busboys officiated at the filling of two water glasses. Maus waved the chlorinated product away with an imperious gesture. "We drink only bottled water," he said, "and we wish to consult the sommelier . . ."

Qwilleran viewed with mounting hunger the dish of **veal and mushrooms,** *aswim in delicate juices. He determined, however, to adhere to his regimen: three bites and quit.*

Veal and Mushrooms

----

1   tablespoon finely chopped chives
1   teaspoon finely chopped celery
3   tablespoons butter or margarine
1¼   cups chicken broth
1½   cups small mushroom buttons
¼   teaspoon paprika
¼   teaspoon dried basil
¼   teaspoon dried tarragon
2   pounds veal, sliced

Preheat oven to 350°. Sauté chives and celery in butter or margarine. Add chicken broth, mushroom buttons, paprika, basil, and tarragon. Stir over low heat until heated through. Place veal in a buttered baking dish. Pour broth mixture over veal. Bake, covered, until almost tender, approximately 25 minutes. Remove cover and bake 20–30 minutes longer to reduce sauce. SERVES 4–6.

After the **braised fennel amandine** *and the tossed salad with nasturtium seeds, and the chestnut puree in meringue nests, and the demitasse, Qwilleran reached in his pocket for his pipe . . .*

Braised Fennel Amandine

2   large fennel bulbs
½   cup water
1   tablespoon + 2 tablespoons butter or margarine
½   teaspoon salt
1   tablespoon all-purpose flour
1   cup half-and-half
2   tablespoons shredded Gruyère cheese
2   tablespoons + ¼ cup grated Parmesan cheese
dash of red pepper
½   cup fine dry bread crumbs
2   tablespoons butter or margarine, melted
¼   cup sliced almonds

Preheat oven to 350°. Cut fennel into 2-inch pieces and place in a saucepan with water and 1 tablespoon of the butter or margarine and salt. Cover and cook over medium heat until tender. Add more water while cooking, if necessary. Drain. Make a sauce by melting remaining 2 tablespoons butter or margarine in a saucepan. Add flour, stirring briskly. Slowly add half-and-half. Stir until thick. Add Gruyère cheese, the 2 tablespoons of Parmesan cheese, and red pepper.

Place fennel in a greased casserole. Pour the sauce over the fennel. Mix the ¼ cup of Parmesan cheese, bread crumbs, and the melted butter or margarine. Sprinkle over the top. Bake 20–25 minutes. Garnish with almonds before serving. SERVES 4–6.

At one stall Maus selected a skinned rabbit, and Qwilleran turned away while the farmer wrapped the red, stiffened carcass in a sheet of newspaper and the white-furred relatives of the deceased looked on with reproach. "Mrs. Marron, I must admit, makes an excellent hasenpfeffer*," Maus explained. "She will prepare the . . . viands this weekend while I attend a gourmet conclave out of town."*

Hasenpfeffer

1   dressed rabbit
3   cups water
1   cup vinegar
½   cup sugar
1   medium onion, sliced
1   teaspoon mixed pickling spices
2   teaspoons salt
¼   teaspoon pepper
3   tablespoons + 2 tablespoons all-purpose flour
3   tablespoons oil

Cut rabbit into serving pieces. Marinate in the water, vinegar, sugar, onion, spices, salt, and pepper several hours or overnight in the refrigerator. Remove rabbit from marinade, reserving 2 cups of the liquid. Coat the rabbit with the 3 tablespoons flour and brown in the oil in a skillet. Add the reserved marinade and simmer until the rabbit is tender. Remove the meat from liquid and add the 2 tablespoons of flour to the mixture to make a gravy. If necessary, add more water to skillet when making gravy. SERVES 4.

At noon when Qwilleran reported downstairs for lunch . . . Mrs. Marron was serving **home-baked beans** *with brown bread . . .*

Home-Baked Beans

1	1-pound bag dried navy beans
6–8	cups cold water for cooking beans
3	strips bacon
1	cup chopped onion
¼	cup molasses
¼	cup brown sugar, packed
1	teaspoon salt
⅛	teaspoon pepper
¾	cup ketchup

Soak beans according to package directions. Drain. Place beans in 6–8 cups cold water. Cook over low heat about 90 minutes or until tender, adding more water if needed. Drain, reserving 1½ cups of the bean liquid. While beans are cooking, fry bacon. Cut into pieces. Sauté onion in a tablespoonful of the bacon grease. Place molasses, sugar, salt, pepper, ketchup, bacon, tender beans, and reserved liquid in a bowl and mix well. Pour into a 1½ quart baking dish or pan and bake, uncovered, at 325° for approximately 1 hour, or until beans begin to brown. SERVES 8.

. . .and leftover ham . . .

Mrs. Marron's Ham

5–8 pound ham, butt portion
3 teaspoons dry mustard
2 cups brown sugar, packed
½ cup dry bread crumbs or cornflake crumbs
3 tablespoons apple juice or white wine
aluminum foil

Preheat oven to 325°. Put ham in roasting pan. Make a "tent" out of a large sheet of aluminum foil by creasing it in half. Place it loosely over the ham. Bake the ham 25 to 30 minutes per pound or until a meat thermometer inserted into center of ham registers 165°. Discard the tent. Make a glaze by mixing the mustard, brown sugar, crumbs, and apple juice or wine. Place it on the ham. Raise the oven temperature to 425° and bake 15 additional minutes. SERVES 6–8.

"What's for dinner?" he [Dan Graham] *demanded.*
"Some nice roast chicken and wild rice."

Roast Chicken

---

1 clove garlic, chopped
2 tablespoons butter or margarine
3–4 pound chicken
4–6 sprigs Italian parsley, rinsed
2 onions, quartered

½ teaspoon dried basil (approximate)
½ teaspoon dried rosemary (approximate)

Preheat oven to 350°. Sauté the garlic in the butter or margarine. Remove the garlic and discard. Rinse the chicken. Place it, breast side up, in a shallow roasting pan. With a sharp knife, cut the membrane between the breast skin and the breast meat. Insert the parsley under the skin and on top of the meat. Arrange parsley so that it looks attractive when it shows through the skin. Brush chicken with garlic-flavored butter or margarine. Place onions into cavity of chicken. Sprinkle chicken lightly with basil and rosemary. Be sure not to obscure the parsley. Roast, uncovered, 20 minutes for each pound of chicken. Baste with any remaining butter or margarine while chicken is roasting. Serve with wild rice. SERVES 4–6.

"And a nice coconut custard pie . . . ."
"And tomorrow a nice rabbit stew," the housekeeper added.

Coconut Custard Pie

Pastry:
½ cup shortening
1½ cups all-purpose flour
½ teaspoon salt
3–4 tablespoons ice water

Cut the shortening into the flour and salt until the mixture is about the size of peas. Add the water a tablespoonful at a time, mixing lightly with a fork. When mixture holds together, gently form it into a ball. On a floured surface, roll into a circle about ¼-inch in thickness to fit into a 9-inch pie pan.

Coconut filling:

- 4 eggs
- 1 cup sugar
- ¼ teaspoon salt
- 1 teaspoon vanilla extract
- 2½ cups milk, scalded
- 1 3½-ounce can flaked coconut
- ¼ cup brown sugar, packed
- 2 tablespoons soft butter or margarine

Preheat oven to 400°. Beat eggs slightly; stir in sugar, salt, and vanilla extract. Gradually stir in milk. Reserve ½ cup coconut for top; add remainder to custard. Pour mixture into unbaked pastry shell. Bake for 25 to 30 minutes or until knife inserted in center comes out clean. Cool. Just before serving, mix reserved coconut, brown sugar, and butter or margarine; sprinkle on top of pie. Broil 2 to 4 minutes or until lightly browned. SERVES 6.

"What's a demonstration dinner?" Qwilleran asked.

"Everybody cooks something at the table." [explained Mrs. Marron]

For the first course Rosemary stood at the head of the table and demonstrated a sixty-second cold soup involving yogurt, cucumbers, dill, and raisins.

Rosemary's Yogurt Soup

- 2½ cups yogurt
- 2 cucumbers, seeds removed
- 1 tablespoon dried dill weed

½　cup raisins

salt and white pepper to taste

Stir yogurt until smooth. Shred cucumbers into fine pieces. Add cucumber, dill weed, raisins, salt, and pepper to the yogurt. If soup is too thick it can be diluted with milk. SERVES 4–6.

Sorrel sautéed **steak** *au poivre . . .*

Sorrel's Steak au Poivre

4　1-inch thick beef top loin, tenderloin, or sirloin steaks

salt to taste

2–4　teaspoons cracked whole black peppercorns

2　onions, chopped

3　cloves garlic, chopped

¼　cup butter or margarine

2　tablespoons Worcestershire sauce

½　cup cream

few drops Tabasco sauce (optional)

¼　cup brandy (optional)

Sprinkle salt on one side of the steaks. Press the cracked peppercorns into the other side using a cleaver or wooden spoon. Sauté the onions and garlic in the butter or margarine until tender. Add the Worcestershire sauce. Place the steaks on the onion and garlic mixture peppercorn side up. Cover and cook slowly to the degree of doneness preferred. Remove from skillet. Stir cream into the skillet drippings to make a sauce. Simmer for one minute. Remove from heat and add Tabasco sauce and/or brandy, if desired. Pour sauce over steaks. SERVES 4.

. . . which was served with Mrs. Marron's potato puffs and asparagus garnished with pimento strips.

Mrs. Marron's Potato Puffs

———

2 cups mashed potatoes
1 cup all-purpose flour
2 teaspoons baking powder
½ teaspoon salt
¼ teaspoon pepper
2 eggs, beaten
cooking oil

Combine potatoes, flour, baking powder, salt, and pepper in a large bowl. Add eggs and stir until well-mixed. Heat cooking oil in large skillet or deep fryer. Drop mixture into the oil by tablespoonsful. Fry until golden brown. Drain on paper towels. Serves 4–6.

Mrs. Marron's Asparagus

———

5 spears of asparagus per person
½ teaspoon salt
lemon juice, ½ teaspoonful for each 5 spears
butter or margarine, melted, 1 teaspoonful for each 5 spears
pimento strips

Snap off the woody ends of the spears. Cook, covered, in a pan of water with salt added. Drain. Mix lemon juice and butter or margarine together. Pour over asparagus. Garnish with pimento strips.

Then Charlotte Roop demonstrated the tossing of a salad. "Dry the greens carefully on a linen towel," she said. "A salad has to be made with love . . . And now the dressing. I add a little Dijon mustard and thyme."

Charlotte Roop's Salad

¼ cup cider vinegar
½ cup extra-light olive oil
2 tablespoons Dijon mustard
½ teaspoon dried thyme
½ teaspoon salt
¼ teaspoon pepper
lettuce of choice

Whisk the vinegar, oil, and mustard together. Add the thyme, salt, and pepper. Whisk vigorously. Wash and dry the greens.

"Be careful not to bruise the leaves. Tear them apart tenderly . . . Toss all together. Gently! Gently! Forty times. Less dressing and more tossing— that's the secret." [Charlotte Roop]

Toss the salad with the dressing as Charlotte did or pour dressing over individual servings. SERVES 4.

For dessert Hixie prepared *cherries jubilee*. "Nothing to it," she said. "Dump the cherries in the chafing dish. Throw in a blob of butter and slosh it around. Then a slurp of cognac. Oops! I slurped too much. And then . . . you light it with a match. Voilà!" The blue flame leaped from the pan, and the company watched the ritual in hypnotized silence.

Hixie Rice's Cherries Jubilee

1   16-ounce can pitted, dark sweet cherries
⅓   cup sugar
1   tablespoon butter or margarine
1   tablespoon cornstarch
½   cup cognac, kirsch, or brandy
vanilla ice cream (optional)

Drain the cherries, reserving ⅓ cup of the syrup. Set cherries aside. Place the syrup, sugar, butter or margarine, and cornstarch in a skillet or chafing dish. Stirring constantly, cook until slightly thick. Add the cherries and, stirring occasionally, heat them through. In another pan, heat the cognac, kirsch, or brandy until very hot, but not boiling. Pour over the cherries and ignite. Serve over ice cream, if desired. SERVES 4.

The Cat Who Played Brahms

Qwilleran, Koko, and Yum Yum go to a secluded cabin owned by "Aunt Fanny," a family friend. As soon as they arrive, strange things begin to happen. They hear footsteps on the roof, crackling in the underbrush, and someone climbing a tree. If that's not enough, Koko keeps punching buttons on the cassette player and playing Brahms.

Boardinghouse Breakfast

Honeydew Melon

Omelette Fines Herbes

Chicken Livers

Cheese Popovers

Coffee

The day had started well enough. He had eaten a good breakfast at his boardinghouse: a wedge of honeydew melon, an omelette fines herbes with sautéed chicken livers, cheese popovers, and three cups of coffee.

Omelette Fines Herbes

---

3 eggs
1 teaspoon water
salt and pepper to taste
1 tablespoon butter or margarine
¼ teaspoon dried parsley
½ teaspoon dried chives
½ teaspoon dried dill weed

Beat eggs, water, salt, and pepper. Heat butter or margarine in a skillet until it begins to bubble. Pour eggs into middle of pan. As eggs cook, keep lifting the edges with a spatula so the uncooked eggs can go underneath. Sprinkle the parsley, chives, and dill weed in the center of the eggs when slightly set. Fold the top third of the omelette over and the bottom third up. SERVES 1–2.

Chicken Livers

7–10   chicken livers
2   tablespoons butter or margarine
salt and pepper to taste
garlic powder to taste

Cut chicken livers in half. Heat butter or margarine in a skillet. Sauté livers in the butter until thoroughly cooked. Season with salt, pepper, and garlic powder. SERVES 4.

Cheese Popovers

---

1   cup all-purpose flour
½   teaspoon salt
1   cup milk
2   eggs
1   tablespoon butter or margarine, melted
½   cup shredded cheddar cheese

Preheat oven to 425°. Grease 8 large or 12 small muffin pans, cupcake pans, or custard cups. Place pans in oven to heat. Put flour and salt in mixing bowl and add milk, eggs, butter or margarine and cheese. Beat well. Fill the pans ½ to ¾ full. Do not overfill. Bake 40 to 45 minutes. Lower the heat to 350° after 20 minutes if popovers are browning too quickly. SERVES 8–12.

À La Carte

At twelve noon Qwilleran bounded up the steps of the grimy limestone
fortress that had once been the county jail but now dispensed food and
drink to the working press . . .

The two newsmen [Riker and Qwilleran] applied themselves to the
lamb curry and the turkey sandwich in silence, indicating deep thought.

Curried Lamb

½   cup chopped onion
¼   cup chopped celery
1   clove garlic, minced
2   tablespoons butter or margarine
2   cups lamb, cooked, cubed
1   teaspoon curry powder
salt and pepper to taste
1   tablespoon Worcestershire sauce
1   14½-ounce can beef broth or 1¾ cups lamb stock
2   tablespoons all-purpose flour
¼   cup water

In a large skillet, sauté onion, celery, and garlic in the butter or margarine. Add the lamb, curry
powder, salt, pepper, Worcestershire sauce, and broth to the sautéed vegetables. Cook about 25
minutes over low heat. Combine the water and flour and stir until smooth. Add flour mixture to
the lamb mixture. Cook until thickened. Serve over rice. (Stock can be made by boiling lamb
bones.) SERVES 4.

Pomegranate juice was poured over ice with a dash of club soda, and a toast was drunk to the condemned building in memory of everything that had happened there.

"It was a way of life we'll never forget," Qwilleran said.

"It was a dream," Rosemary added.

Pomegranate Juice and Club Soda

8 ounces pomegranate juice
1 ounce club soda
cracked ice

Place ice in 8-ounce glass. Pour pomegranate juice over ice and add club soda. Stir.

In her chesty voice she [Aunt Fanny] said: "I have some divine **cinnamon buns** . . . You adored cinnamon buns when you were a little boy."

Divine Cinnamon Buns

1 cup rolled oats
½ cup + 1 cup sugar
3½–4 cups all-purpose flour
1 package dry yeast
1 teaspoon salt
1 cup milk

½   cup water

¼   cup sour cream

3   tablespoons + 1 tablespoon shortening

1egg

1   tablespoon cinnamon

¾   cup butter or margarine, melted

Mix rolled oats, ½ cup sugar, 2 cups of the flour, yeast, and salt in a large bowl. In a saucepan, slowly heat milk, water, sour cream, and 3 tablespoons shortening until very warm—120 to 130°. Do not heat too rapidly or sour cream may curdle. Add warm liquid to flour mixture. Blend, at low speed, using electric mixer, until moistened. Add egg and beat 2 minutes at medium speed. Stir in as much of remaining flour by hand as needed to make a soft dough. Place in a greased bowl. Brush top with remaining 1 tablespoon melted shortening. Place plastic wrap loosely on top of dough. Cover with towel and allow to rise until double in size, approximately one hour. Punch down. Divide into 18 balls and place in greased muffin tins. Cover and let rise until double in size again, approximately 45 minutes. Bake at 375° 15 to 20 minutes. Let the buns cool for 5 minutes. Place the remaining 1 cup sugar and cinnamon in a plastic bag and shake to mix. Dip buns in melted butter, place in bag, and shake in sugar-cinnamon mixture. MAKES 18 LARGE OR 36 MINI BUNS.

*"What are these **pasties** everyone advertises?"*

"It's like a turnover filled with meat and potatoes and turnips. Pasties are traditional up here. The miners used to carry pasties in their lunch buckets."

"Where's a good place to try one?" . . .

"For a good hats-off place you could try a little bistro at the Cannery Mall, called the Nasty Pasty. A bit of perverse humor, I guess. . . ."

Qwilleran said he would prefer real north country atmosphere.

"Right. So here's what you do. Drive west along the shore for about a

mile. You'll see a big electric sign that says FOO. The D dropped off about three years ago. It's a dump, but they're famous for pasties, and it's strictly hats-on. . . . "

When Qwilleran's two pasties arrived they completely filled two large oval platters. Each of the crusty turnovers was a foot wide and three inches thick.

Foo Pasty

1   pound lean ground beef
1   cup finely diced turnips
½   cup minced onion
1   teaspoon salt
½   teaspoon black pepper
1   beaten egg yolk

Pastry:

2   cups all-purpose flour
1   teaspoon salt
½   cup shortening
¼   cup milk
¼   cup water

Preheat oven to 350°. Using hands, mix together beef, turnips, onion, salt, and pepper. Set aside. Make pastry by mixing or sifting flour and salt together. In a small saucepan, bring the shortening, milk, and water to a boil. Make a well in the flour mixture and pour in the hot mixture. Mix with a large spoon until smooth. On a floured surface, roll out half of the dough into a 12-inch circle. Place half the meat mixture off-center in the pastry round. Moisten the edges of the pastry with water. Fold the dough over to make a semicircle. Crimp edges together with a fork. Make small slits in the pasty with the point of a knife. Brush pasty with egg yolk. Repeat with remaining dough and filling. Place on ungreased cookie sheet. Bake for 60 minutes. Serve hot or cold. SERVES 4.

"No doubt you will be seeing her [Fanny] during the summer?" [Goodwinter asked]

"Yes, she promised to come up for lunch, and I have a rain check on a steak dinner in Pickax." [said Qwilleran]

"Ah, yes, we all know Fanny's steak dinners," Goodwinter said with a humorous grimace. "She promises steak, but when the time comes she serves scrambled eggs. One forgives her eccentricities because of her—ah—energetic involvement in the community."

Aunt Fanny's Steak Dinner

4 eggs
3 tablespoons cream
salt and pepper to taste
dash of dried dill weed
2 teaspoons butter or margarine

Vigorously beat eggs, cream, salt, pepper, and dill weed with a fork. Heat butter or margarine in skillet; add the eggs. Stir occasionally until eggs are cooked to the degree of doneness preferred. SERVES 2.

"[Tom,] *Bring the picnic basket from the car before you leave . . . I've brought some* **egg salad sandwiches** *and a thermos of coffee with that marvelous* cream." [said Aunt Fanny] *"We'll sit on the porch and enjoy the lake. The temperature is perfect. Now where are those intelligent cats I've heard so much about?"*

Egg Salad Sandwiches

6 hard-boiled eggs, chopped
1 tablespoon sweet pickle relish
1 tablespoon finely chopped celery
½ teaspoon Dijon mustard
mayonnaise or salad dressing
salt and pepper to taste
butter, room temperature
6 slices whole wheat bread

Combine eggs, relish, celery, and mustard. Add enough mayonnaise or salad dressing to moisten to a good consistency for spreading. Add salt and pepper. Butter 3 slices bread, spread with egg salad, and top with remaining slices. SERVES 3.

"Will you settle for a dinner date?" [asked Qwilleran]

"Make it a quick lunch, and I can go right now," she [Melinda Goodwinter] said, consulting her watch. *"I never refuse lunch with an interesting older man. Do you like* **pasties***?"*

"They'd be okay if they had flaky pastry, a little sauce, and less turnip."

"Then you'll love the Nasty Pasty. Let's go . . ."

The pasties were a success: flaky, juicy, turnipless, and of comfortable size.

Nasty Pasty Pasty

½   pound ground sirloin
¼   teaspoon salt
⅛   teaspoon black pepper
¼   cup chopped onion
½   teaspoon Worcestershire sauce
⅛   teaspoon ground nutmeg
⅛   cup beef beef broth, double strength, undiluted
1   tablespoon finely chopped fresh parsley
1   tablespoon dried bread crumbs
1   egg, slightly beaten, to brush pastry

Pastry:

2   cups all-purpose flour
1   teaspoon salt
2   teaspoons sugar
⅔   cup shortening
2   teaspoons white vinegar
5–7   tablespoons cold water

Preheat oven to 350°. In a medium bowl, mix together sirloin, salt, pepper, onion, Worcestershire sauce, nutmeg, beef broth, parsley, and bread crumbs. Use hands for uniform blending. Set aside. In another bowl, combine flour, salt, and sugar. Cut in shortening until crumbly. Gradually add vinegar and as much water as necessary to form a ball of dough. Roll out pastry on a floured surface. Cut into 6-inch rounds. Shape the meat mixture into 6 four-inch logs. Place each meat log in the center of each pastry round and moisten the edges of pastry with water. Bring sides of pastry up over meat, crimping decoratively on top with fingers. Brush pasty with beaten egg. Make small slits in sides of pasty. Bake on ungreased cookie sheet for 40–45 minutes. Serve hot or cold. MAKES 6.

The Cat Who Played Post Office

Qwilleran becomes a millionaire and even moves into a mansion. Still, he's not sure what to do with all that money. Koko leaves clues to help Qwill solve the case of the missing housemaid.

Klingenshoen Mansion Dinner Party

Escargot

Terrine of Pheasant

Jellied Watercress Consommé

Salmon Croquettes

Lamb Bûcheronne with Potatoes and Mushrooms

Asparagus Vinaigrette Salad

Raspberry Trifle

❧

"If I decide to give a dinner party, will you consent to be my hostess?"
[asked Qwilleran]

"Or anything else, lover," she [Melinda] *said with a green-eyed wink . . .*
"You should have something elegant: six courses, starting with **escargot** *. . .*
a butler serving cocktails in the solarium. . . two footmen to serve in the din-
ing room . . . a string trio going crazy behind the potted palms."

In the dining room, crystal and silver glittered on white damask, and two
towering candelabra flanked a Victorian epergne, its branches filled with
flowers, fruit, nuts, and mints . . . Sixteen wax candles were burning in
the silver candelabra, and twenty-four electric candles were aglow in the
staghorn chandeliers, all of this against a rich background of linenfold
paneling and drawn velvet draperies.

Escargot

6 green onions, chopped fine
½ cup white wine + enough to add to escargot pans
24 snail shells
1 7-ounce can snails
¼ cup butter or margarine, softened
2 tablespoons finely chopped parsley
1 clove garlic, minced
1 teaspoon dried basil
bread crumbs
wine
French bread, sliced

Preheat oven to 400°. Sauté green onions in ½ cup of white wine for 3 minutes. Spoon a portion of onions into each shell. Rinse snails and cut in half to make 24 pieces. Place snails in shells. Mix together butter or margarine, parsley, garlic, and basil. Seal the opening of the shell with the butter or margarine mixture and then dip sealed opening in bread crumbs. Place shells in escargot pans and add 1 tablespoon of wine to each pan. Bake for 10 minutes. Serve on slice of French bread to soak up the butter. SERVES 8.

... *"We ought to serve foods indigenous to this area, starting with terrine of pheasant..."* [said Melinda]

Terrine of Pheasant

½	pound thinly sliced bacon (approximate)
2	tablespoons dried parsley
2	tablespoons chopped onion
1	pound veal scallops
½	teaspoon salt
¼	teaspoon pepper
½	teaspoon dried basil
1	pound pheasant or chicken breast
1½	cups white wine

Preheat oven to 300°. Line the bottom and sides of a baking pan (approximately 9-inch by 5-inch and 3-inch deep) with raw, overlapping bacon strips. Sprinkle with a little of the parsley and onion. Pound the veal scallops until they are very thin. Place a layer of veal over the bacon. Season with salt, pepper, and basil. Pound pheasant or chicken breast until very thin. Make a layer over the veal. Add more parsley and onion. Continue layering the veal, salt, pepper, and basil; then the pheasant or chicken, parsley and onion until all are used. Cover the top with additional bacon strips. Add enough wine to fill to the top of the meat. Put the pan in a larger pan of water. Bake about 2 hours. After the meat is finished baking, remove from pan of water, and cover it with aluminum foil or plastic wrap. Put a heavy object on it to press it together until it cools. Refrigerate. Slice to serve. Serve cold. SERVES 6–8.

". . . and *jellied watercress consommé*. There's a secret cove on the Ittibittiwassee—accessible only by canoe—where one can find watercress. Do you canoe?"

Jellied Watercress Consommé

2 envelopes unflavored gelatin
½ cup water
2 cups tomato juice
2 14½-ounce cans chicken broth
¼ teaspoon lemon juice
salt and pepper to taste
¼ teaspoon Worcestershire sauce
1 cup watercress, chopped
watercress for garnish

Soak the gelatin in the water for a few minutes. Heat the tomato juice, chicken broth, lemon juice, salt, and pepper to boiling. Add the gelatin and cool to lukewarm. Add the Worcestershire sauce and watercress. Put into 2-quart bowl and chill until firm. Consommé may be beaten slightly with a fork before serving. Garnish with more watercress. SERVES 4–6.

"How about Chinook salmon croquettes for the fish course?"

Salmon Croquettes

---

2 cups canned salmon, drained
2 cups mashed potatoes (can use instant type prepared according to package directions)
2 tablespoons ketchup
1 tablespoon dried parsley
2 eggs
½ teaspoon salt
⅛ teaspoon pepper
fine, dry bread crumbs or finely crushed cracker crumbs
milk (optional)
cooking oil

Mix the salmon, potatoes, ketchup, parsley, 1 of the eggs, salt, and pepper. If mixture is too moist to form balls, add bread crumbs. If too dry, add a little milk. Shape into croquettes (balls). Beat second egg. Dip croquettes into egg and then in bread or cracker crumbs. Fry in oil in skillet or deep fryer until browned. MAKES 10–12 CROQUETTES.

"The entree could be lamb bûcheronne with tiny Moose County pota-toes and mushrooms. It's too dry to find morels."

Lamb Bûcheronne with Potatoes and Mushrooms

Lamb:

5–6 pound leg of lamb
garlic salt

Preheat oven to 375°. Sprinkle lamb with garlic salt. Roast 2½ hours or until meat thermometer reads 175° for medium or 180° for well-done. Slice and keep warm.

Gravy:
- ¼ cup flour
- 3 tablespoons drippings from pan in which lamb was roasted
- 2 cups water (approximate)
- salt and pepper to taste

Remove lamb from pan and make gravy by adding flour to drippings. Over low heat, add water to make gravy of desired consistency, stirring constantly. Add salt and pepper.

Mushroom mixture:
- 6 cups sliced fresh mushrooms, variety of choice
- ¼ cup chopped onion
- 2 cloves garlic, chopped
- ¼ cup butter or margarine
- ¼ cup chopped fresh parsley
- ¼ cup bread crumbs
- salt and pepper to taste

Sauté the mushrooms, onion, and garlic in butter or margarine. Remove from heat. Add the parsley, bread crumbs, salt and pepper. Stir.

Potatoes:
- 12-15 tiny potatoes
- 2 tablespoons butter
- salt and pepper to taste

Peel potatoes. Boil until tender but firm. Slice and brown in butter. Add salt and pepper. Place sliced lamb on serving plate. Arrange the potatoes and mushrooms around lamb. Serve with gravy. SERVES 6.

*"Then a salad of homegrown **asparagus vinaigrette**."*

Asparagus Vinaigrette Salad

Vinaigrette:

- ⅓   cup olive oil or vegetable oil
- 2½   tablespoons white vinegar
- 1   tablespoon chopped fresh parsley
- 1   tablespoon chopped fresh chives
- 1   tablespoon finely chopped onion
- ¼   teaspoon pepper
- ¼   teaspoon salt

Vigorously whisk together all ingredients.

> 5   spears of asparagus per person
> salt to taste
> water
> lettuce of choice

Steam or boil the asparagus in salted water until tender but not mushy. Drain, chill, arrange on lettuce and serve with vinaigrette.

"Don't forget dessert. Preferably not French-fried ice cream." [said Qwilleran]

*"How about a wild **raspberry trifle**?"* [asked Melinda]

Raspberry Trifle

1   4.6–ounce package vanilla pudding mix
3   cups milk to prepare pudding
1   10-ounce package frozen raspberries or 2½ cups fresh raspberries
½   cup + 2 tablespoons water
⅔   cup sugar
2   tablespoons cornstarch
1½   cups whipping cream
2   tablespoons powdered sugar
½   teaspoon almond or vanilla extract
24   ladyfingers
raspberry jelly
⅓   cup rum or orange juice
almond slices or slivers

Prepare the pudding mix as per instructions on box. Cool, covered with plastic wrap to keep film from forming. Make raspberry filling by placing raspberries in a saucepan with ½ cup water. Place over medium heat, stirring frequently to crush berries. Bring to a gentle boil. Remove from heat and strain seeds, reserving liquid. Return liquid to pan; add sugar, stir over medium heat until sugar dissolves. Add 2 tablespoons water to the cornstarch. Add the cornstarch to the juice. Continue to cook over medium heat until thickened and clear. Cool. Whip cream, adding powdered sugar and vanilla or almond extract. Mix half of the whipped cream with the cooled pudding. Split the ladyfingers. Spread with jelly. Put the halves back together. Place a layer of ladyfingers on bottom of a glass bowl. Sprinkle with rum or orange juice. Spoon half the raspberry filling over the ladyfingers. Spoon half of the pudding and whipped cream mixture over the raspberry filling. Make another layer of ladyfingers. Repeat layers. Top with remaining whipped cream. Garnish with almonds. SERVES 6.

À La Carte

*At the club, where the air conditioner was out of commission, they ordered corned beef sandwiches, **gin and tonic** for Riker, and iced tea for Qwilleran.*

Gin and Tonic

cracked ice
½   lime, juiced
1½   ounces gin
quinine water

Place ice in 12-ounce glass. Add lime juice, gin, and quinine water. Stir.

"Dear Qwill,

*. . . Drop in some afternoon. I've been picking **wild blueberries for pies**. [note from] Mildred Hanstable."*

The Hanstable summer cottage overlooked the lake, and an umbrella table was set up for the repast.

"Mildred, your blueberry pie is perfection," Qwilleran said. "Not too viscous, not too liquescent."

She laughed with pleasure.

Perfection Blueberry Pie

Pastry:

1¼	cups shortening
3	cups all-purpose flour
1	teaspoon salt
1	egg, well beaten
3–5	tablespoons water
1	tablespoon vinegar

Cut shortening into flour and salt using pastry blender or fork. Combine egg, 3 tablespoons water, and vinegar. Pour liquid into flour mixture all at once. Blend with spoon until all flour is moistened, adding more water, if necessary. Divide into 2 equal portions. Roll one portion into a circle to fit into a 9-inch pie pan and line the pan. Reserve second portion for top crust. (This crust is very easy to handle. Can be rerolled without toughening.)

Pie filling:

1	cup sugar
½	cup all-purpose flour
1	tablespoon lemon juice
1	tablespoon butter or margarine
5	cups blueberries
½	tablespoon sugar
⅛	teaspoon ground cinnamon

Preheat oven to 400°. Stir sugar and flour together in a saucepan. Add lemon juice, butter or margarine, and 3 cups berries. Stirring constantly, bring to a boil over medium-high heat. Boil for two minutes or until thickened. Remove from heat and stir in remaining blueberries. Cool completely. Pour blueberry mixture into unbaked pastry shell. Roll out remaining pastry and place over blueberries. Crimp to seal edges. Make small slits in top crust to let steam escape. Piecrust can be latticed by cutting the top crust into 1-inch strips and weaving lattice design over filling. Mix the sugar and cinnamon together. Spritz the top crust with ice water and then sprinkle with the cinnamon and sugar mixture. Bake 30–40 minutes. SERVES 6.

. . . Mrs. Cobb was planning lamb stew with dumplings *for dinner, with her famous coconut cake for dessert.*

Lamb Stew with Dumplings

1½ pounds lamb shoulder, diced
⅓ cup all-purpose flour (approximate)
3 tablespoons shortening or oil
2½ cups water + ¼ cup cold water
1 teaspoon salt
⅛ teaspoon pepper
1 bay leaf
5 potatoes, peeled and cut into large pieces
1 onion, chopped
5 carrots, sliced
2 tablespoons + 2 cups biscuit mix
¾ cup milk

Place meat and flour in a bag and shake to coat meat. Brown meat in the shortening or oil. Add 1 cup of the water. Cover and simmer over low heat for 40 minutes. Add salt, pepper, bay leaf, potatoes, onion, and carrots. Add 1½ cups of water and simmer about 40 minutes or until tender. Remove bay leaf. If desired, thicken by adding the 2 tablespoons biscuit mix and the remaining ¼ cup cold water. Make dumplings by mixing the 2 cups biscuit mix with milk. Stir thoroughly; immediately drop by tablespoonsful onto simmering stew. Cook uncovered for 10 minutes. Cover and cook 10 minutes longer. SERVES 6–8.

Mrs. Cobb quickly filled two mugs from the coffee maker and set them on the table, together with a plate of doughnuts.

Mrs. Cobb's Doughnuts

2 eggs, beaten
1¼ cups sugar
¼ cup shortening, melted
1 cup mashed potatoes
1 teaspoon lemon zest
4 cups all-purpose flour
1 tablespoon baking powder
½ teaspoon baking soda
½ teaspoon nutmeg
1 teaspoon salt
⅓ cup buttermilk
oil for frying

Beat eggs with sugar and shortening. Add mashed potatoes and lemon zest. Sift or mix flour, baking powder, baking soda, nutmeg, and salt together. Add the flour mixture to the potato mixture, alternating with the buttermilk. Place the dough on a floured surface. Roll to ¼ inch thickness. Cut with doughnut cutter. Drop doughnuts into oil heated to 365° in a deep fat fryer or deep skillet. Fry until brown on both sides, turning doughnuts over once. Remove and drain on paper towels. Glaze as described below. MAKES ABOUT 2 DOZEN.

Glaze:

1   cup sugar
½   cup butter or margarine
½   cup milk
3   cups powdered sugar
¼   teaspoon salt
½   teaspoon vanilla extract

Put sugar, butter or margarine, and milk in a saucepan. Heat and stir until mixture boils. Boil one minute. Remove from heat and add powdered sugar, salt, and vanilla extract. Stir until smooth. Dip tops of doughnuts in warm glaze and drain on a wire rack.

The housekeeper [Mrs. Cobb] served lunch in the cheerful breakfast room, where William and Mary banister-back chairs surrounded a dark oak table, and yellow and green chintz covered the walls and draped the windows. "Best **macaroni and cheese** *I ever tasted," Qwilleran announced.*

Mrs. Cobb's Macaroni and Cheese

6   cups water
1¾   cups elbow macaroni
⅓   cup chopped onion
1   tablespoon + 4 tablespoons butter or margarine, melted
1   teaspoon dry mustard
1   teaspoon salt
⅛   teaspoon black pepper
⅛   teaspoon red pepper

2 cups + 1 cup shredded extra sharp cheddar cheese
1 cup shredded mozzarella cheese
½ cup sour cream
¼ cup half-and-half
3 eggs, beaten slightly
1–3 tablespoons dry white wine (Mrs. Cobb's secret ingredient)

Preheat oven to 350°. Bring water to a boil. Add macaroni, stirring occasionally to separate elbows. Bring to a boil again; reduce heat to medium. Cook, uncovered, until tender—about 10 minutes. Drain. Sauté onion in 1 tablespoon of the butter or margarine. Stir onion while adding the mustard, salt, and peppers. Set aside. In another bowl, combine 2 cups cheddar cheese, mozzarella cheese, 4 tablespoons melted butter or margarine, sour cream, half-and-half, and eggs. Combine macaroni, onion mixture, cheese mixture, and wine. Place in greased casserole dish. Sprinkle top with 1 cup cheddar cheese. Bake 35 minutes. SERVES 6.

"Sorry to be late," Qwilleran apologized as he sat down to a plate of real buttermilk pancakes . . .

Real Buttermilk Pancakes

2 cups buttermilk
2 eggs, beaten
1½ cups all-purpose flour
1 tablespoon sugar
½ teaspoon salt
1 teaspoon baking soda
1½ teaspoons baking powder
3 tablespoons butter or margarine, melted
oil

Mix the buttermilk and eggs together. Sift or mix the flour, sugar, salt, baking soda, and baking powder together. Combine the buttermilk mixture and the flour mixture. Add the butter or margarine. Mix with as little stirring as possible. Batter will have lumps in it. Fry on a hot, greased griddle or in a skillet with a little oil. Makes about fifteen 5-inch pancakes. SERVES 4–5.

"... I'll grab a hamburger somewhere."

"You don't need to do that, Mr. Qwilleran. I bought four beautiful loin chops and some big Idaho bakers, and I could put them in the oven before I go. I thought maybe you'd like to ask someone over." [answered Mrs. Cobb]

"Good idea! I'll invite Junior. I owe him one ..."

They ate their pork chops at the massive kitchen table.

"According to Mrs. Cobb," Qwilleran pointed out, "this is probably a sixteenth-century table from a Spanish monastery."

Baked Pork Chops

4   pork loin chops
2   tablespoons oil
⅓   cup diced celery
3   tablespoons brown sugar
1   tablespoon lemon juice
½   teaspoon prepared mustard
2   tablespoons ketchup
1   tablespoon Worcestershire sauce

2   tablespoons chopped onion

1   small clove garlic, chopped

salt and pepper to taste

Preheat oven to 325°. Brown chops in oil. Place in shallow greased baking dish. Mix the rest of the ingredients. Pour over the pork chops. Cover tightly. Bake for 1 hour. Uncover and bake 30 minutes more or until chops are tender. SERVES 4–6.

"She's [Mrs. Cobb] a swell cook," Junior said. "You're lucky."
"She made fresh peach pie for our dessert." [said Qwilleran]

Fresh Peach Cobbler Pie

Pastry:

1   stick butter or margarine, melted

1   cup all-purpose flour

1   tablespoon sugar

Mix butter or margarine, flour, and sugar together with fork. Pat dough, with floured fingertips, into 9-inch pie pan.

Peach filling:

5   cups sliced fresh peaches

¾   cup sugar

2   heaping tablespoons quick-cooking tapioca

2   tablespoons lemon juice

2½   tablespoons butter or margarine

Topping:

- 4 tablespoons brown sugar, packed
- 4 tablespoons all-purpose flour
- ½ teaspoon cinnamon
- 3 tablespoons butter or margarine
- ⅔ cup chopped pecans or sliced almonds

Preheat oven to 350°. Combine peaches, sugar, tapioca, lemon juice, and butter or margarine. Place in unbaked pie shell. To make topping, combine brown sugar, flour, cinnamon, and butter or margarine. Mix well. Add nuts. Mix lightly. Place on peaches. Bake for 40–45 minutes. The bottom of the crust will soften slightly, creating a cobblerlike texture. Filling may be used in an unbaked, commercially prepared pastry shell to make a traditional peach pie. SERVES 6.

At long last Mrs. Cobb announced a bit of lunch in the kitchen. "Only left-over vichyssoise and a tuna sandwich," she said. . . .

"I wonder how many Castilian monks sat at this table four centuries ago and had broiled open-face tuna sandwiches with Dijon mustard and capers. They're delicious, Mrs. Cobb." [Qwilleran told her]

Vichyssoise

- 1 medium onion, chopped
- 1–2 leeks, chopped
- 2 tablespoons butter or margarine
- 3 potatoes, peeled and cut into small pieces
- 2 14½-ounce cans chicken broth
- ½ teaspoon salt

¼   teaspoon pepper
1½   cups light cream
       chopped chives

Sauté onion and leeks in butter or margarine. Place the potatoes, broth, salt, and pepper in a saucepan. Add onion and leeks. Cook over low heat until potatoes are tender. Put into a blender and blend until smooth. Chill. Add the cream. Stir well. Garnish with chives. Serve chilled. SERVES 6.

Open-Face Tuna Sandwiches

1   12-ounce can tuna, drained
1   cup finely chopped celery
3   hard-boiled eggs, chopped
1   medium onion, chopped
2   teaspoons Dijon mustard
2   teaspoons mayonnaise
4   teaspoons sweet pickle relish
2   teaspoons sugar
2   teaspoons capers
6   slices lightly buttered bread

Mix all ingredients together except bread. Place tuna mixture on the bread slices. Broil on top oven rack until heated through. Serves 4–6.

The Cat Who Knew Shakespeare

The local newspaper publisher is dead. Is it an accident? Qwilleran and Koko beg to differ. They think it might be murder, but how to prove it? That is the question!

Cozy Fireside Dinner for Two

Sweet Potato Casserole

❖

Mrs. Cobb's Baked Ham

❖

Ginger-Pear Salad

❖

Milk Chocolate Mousse

"If you want to have someone in for dinner," Mrs. Cobb said [to Qwilleran]. . . . *"I'll set the marquetry table in the library with a Maderia cloth and candles and everything. It will be nice and cozy for two . . ."*

In the library the lamps were lighted, logs were blazing in the fireplace, and the table was laid with a dazzling display of porcelain, crystal, and silver. The four walls of books were accented by marble busts of Homer, Dante, and Shakespeare.

*"I'll put a **sweet potato casserole** in the oven."* [offered Mrs. Cobb]

Sweet Potato Casserole

3 cups mashed cooked sweet potatoes
1 cup sugar
½ teaspoon salt
2 eggs, beaten
3 tablespoons + 3 tablespoons butter or margarine, melted
½ cup milk
1 teaspoon vanilla extract
1 cup brown sugar
⅓ cup all-purpose flour
1 cup chopped pecans

Preheat oven to 350°. Mix sweet potatoes, sugar, salt, eggs, 3 tablespoons of the butter or margarine, milk, and vanilla extract. Place in a greased 1½-quart casserole dish. Mix brown sugar, flour, pecans, and the remaining 3 tablespoons of butter or margarine. Spread on top of sweet potato mixture. Bake for 30 minutes. SERVES 6.

"You can serve the baked ham . . ."

Mrs. Cobb's Baked Ham

—————

3   cups all-purpose flour
2   tablespoons ground cloves
2   tablespoons cinnamon
2   tablespoons dry mustard
1   teaspoon pepper
1¼   cups water or apple juice
5–7   pound ham, butt end

Mix flour, cloves, cinnamon, dry mustard, and pepper together. Add enough of the water or juice to make a stiff dough. Roll into an oblong sheet. Cover all of the ham with the dough. Put the ham in a cold oven and then set the temperature to 350°. Bake 20 minutes per pound. Let ham cool slightly in the crust. Remove crust and discard. Slice ham to serve. SERVES 10–12.

". . . and I'll make the ginger-pear salad you like . . ."

Ginger-Pear Salad

—————

Ginger-Pear puree:
2   cups fresh peeled, cored, and cubed pears
2   teaspoons grated gingerroot

1   tablespoon sugar
1   teaspoon lemon juice
    water

Place pear in saucepan. Combine gingerroot, sugar, and lemon juice and pour over pears. Cook over low heat until pears are soft—5 to 8 minutes. Depending on juiciness of pears, it may be necessary to add 2–4 tablespoons of water while cooking. Puree in a blender.

3   fresh pears (or 6 canned pear halves)
2   cups water
1   tablespoon sugar
3   ounces cream cheese
¼   cup whipping cream, whipped
1   teaspoon sugar
⅛   teaspoon vanilla extract
1   tablespoon chopped pistachio nuts

If using fresh pears, peel, halve, and core carefully. Then place in a saucepan, cover with water, add sugar, and simmer for 10 minutes. Remove pears from pan; drain and pat dry. Beat cream cheese until fluffy; add whipped cream, sugar, and vanilla extract. Blend until smooth. Place cream cheese mixture in scooped out core indentation of pears. Pour pureed pears over top and then sprinkle with nuts. SERVES 6.

Mrs. Cobb had left the coffee maker plugged in and pots of chocolate mousse in the refrigerator, and the meal ended pleasantly.

Milk Chocolate Mousse

1 quart half-and-half
1 cup sugar
½ cup all-purpose flour
3 tablespoons cocoa
⅛ teaspoon salt
2 eggs
1 teaspoon + ¼ teaspoon vanilla extract
1 cup whipping cream
2 tablespoons powdered sugar

Heat half-and-half in top of double boiler. Sift or mix sugar, flour, cocoa, and salt together, removing any lumps. Place cocoa mixture in medium-sized bowl. Add 1–1½ cups of hot half-and-half to cocoa mixture, stirring constantly. Return to the rest of the half-and-half in double boiler and cook, stirring, until thickened. Beat eggs until frothy; add 1 teaspoon vanilla extract. Blend small amount of hot mixture into eggs and then return all to the double boiler. Cook for 1 minute longer. Pour mixture into a bowl and cover the top with cling wrap. Refrigerate until thoroughly cooled. Beat whipping cream until stiff peaks form. Mix in the powdered sugar and ¼ teaspoon vanilla extract. Gently fold the whipped cream into the chocolate mixture. Place in individual pots. Chill until serving time. SERVES 6.

À La Carte

On the evening of November fifth, Jim Qwilleran was relaxing in his comfortable library in the company of friends. A mood of contentment prevailed. They had dined well, the housekeeper having prepared clam chowder and **escalopes of veal Casimir**.

Escalopes of Veal Casimir

8 artichoke bottoms
butter or margarine
8 thin slices veal
salt and pepper to taste
4–6 carrots, cut into 3-inch julienne strips
2 tablespoons all-purpose flour
2 cups half-and-half
paprika

Preheat oven to 325°. Sauté the artichoke bottoms in butter or margarine. Place in a baking pan. Then sauté the veal, adding more butter or margarine, if necessary. Season with salt and pepper. Place 1 slice of veal on each artichoke bottom. On top of each slice of veal, place strips of carrots. Bake, covered, until meat is tender, approximately 30 minutes. Remove and place on warm serving plate. Add flour to drippings in pan. Stir over low heat; slowly adding half-and-half to make a sauce. Season with additional salt and pepper, if desired, and paprika. Pour sauce over veal and serve. SERVES 6–8.

Hixie seated him [Qwilleran] near the turning mill wheel. "This is considered a choice table," she said, "although the motion of the wheel makes some of our customers seasick. It's the creaking that drives me up the wall . . ." She handed him a menu. "The lamb shank with ratatouille is good today."

Lamb Shank with Ratatouille

---

4   lamb shanks

flour

oil

2   cloves of garlic, minced

1   large onion, chopped

1   green pepper, chopped

1   medium eggplant, unpeeled, cut into ½-inch strips, then into large chunks

3   medium tomatoes, peeled, chopped

2   medium zucchini, unpeeled, cut into ½-inch strips, then into large chunks

salt and pepper to taste

paprika to taste

¼   teaspoon dried thyme

¼   teaspoon dried oregano

Preheat oven to 350°. Dredge lamb shanks in flour. Brown in the oil. Place in a baking dish with a little water, cover, and bake about 1 hour. Then add the garlic, onion, pepper, eggplant, tomatoes, and zucchini. Sprinkle with salt, pepper, paprika, thyme, and oregano. Cover; bake an additional hour or until lamb is tender. SERVES 4.

For dinner that night Mrs. Cobb served beef Stroganoff and poppy-seed noodles, and after second helpings and a wedge of pumpkin pie, Qwilleran took some out-of-town newspapers and two new magazines into the library.

Beef Stroganoff

1½   pounds sirloin steak

1   tablespoon + 2 tablespoons all-purpose flour
½   teaspoon salt
⅛   teaspoon pepper
2   tablespoons + 2 tablespoons butter or margarine
1   cup tomato or vegetable juice
1   cup water
1   small clove garlic, minced
½   cup chopped onion
1   4-ounce jar sliced mushrooms, drained, or 1 cup sliced fresh mushrooms
1   cup sour cream
2   tablespoons dry white wine (optional)
1   recipe poppy-seed noodles

Slice beef across the grain into strips about ½-inch wide and 3 inches long. Combine 1 tablespoon flour with salt and pepper in a plastic bag. Add meat slices and shake bag to coat. Heat 2 tablespoons of the butter or margarine in a large skillet; add meat and brown quickly on both sides. Pour tomato or vegetable juice and water over meat. Cover tightly and simmer until tender, about 90 minutes. When meat is nearly tender, in a separate small skillet, melt remaining 2 tablespoons butter or margarine. Sauté garlic, onion, and mushrooms. Add 2 tablespoons flour. Stir until smooth. Slowly add ½ cup tomato liquid from meat, stirring constantly. Stir onion mixture into large skillet containing meat and remaining tomato liquid. If there is not 1 cup of liquid left, stir in additional water to make approximately 1 cup. Fold in sour cream and wine, if desired. Heat through, but do not boil. Serve over poppy-seed noodles. SERVES 4.

Poppy-Seed Noodles

6 cups water
1 teaspoon salt
2 cups noodles
¼ cup butter or margarine, melted
1½ tablespoons poppy seeds
⅛ teaspoon pepper

Bring the water to a boil. Add the salt and the noodles. Boil 8 minutes or longer to desired tenderness. Drain and return to the pan. Add the melted butter or margarine, poppy seeds, and pepper. Mix well.

Mrs. Cobb's Pumpkin Pie

Pastry:
5 tablespoons shortening
1 cup all-purpose flour
1 tablespoon powdered sugar
½ teaspoon salt
⅛ teaspoon cinnamon
3 tablespoons ice water or just enough to hold dough together

Cut shortening into flour, powdered sugar, salt, and cinnamon with pastry blender or fork until mixture looks like a coarse meal. Add water a tablespoonful at a time, mixing lightly into flour mixture with a fork. Gently form into a ball. Roll out into a circle ¼ inch in thickness on floured surface. Place in 9-inch pie pan. Chill 5–10 minutes before adding pumpkin filling.

Pumpkin filling:
- ½ cup sugar
- ¼ cup brown sugar, packed
- ½ teaspoon salt
- 2 teaspoons pumpkin pie spice
- 2 eggs, beaten
- 1 15-ounce can pumpkin
- 1½ cups half-and-half or evaporated milk
- 1 cup sweetened whipped cream or whipped topping (optional)

Preheat oven to 425°. Mix sugars, salt, and spice in a small bowl. In another bowl, mix eggs and pumpkin. Add sugar mixture. Slowly stir in half-and-half or evaporated milk. Pour into unbaked pastry shell. Bake at 425° for 15 minutes. Then reduce heat and bake at 350° for about 45 minutes or until knife inserted in center comes out clean. Garnish with whipped cream or whipped topping, if desired. Serves 6.

" . . . There'll be a brief business meeting and refreshments." [said Mrs. Cobb]

"I hope you didn't bake seventy-five dozen cookies for those shameless cookie hounds," Qwilleran said. "I suspect most of them attend meetings because of your *lemon-coconut bars*."

Mrs Cobb's Legendary Lemon-Coconut Bars

¾ cup butter or margarine
½ cup powdered sugar
¼ teaspoon salt
1 teaspoon vanilla extract
2 cups all-purpose flour
4 eggs
2 cups sugar
½ cup bottled lemon juice
1 cup coconut
powdered sugar

Preheat oven to 350°. Cream butter or margarine, powdered sugar, and salt. Stir in vanilla extract and flour. Press into 9-inch by 13-inch baking pan. Bake 20 minutes. Remove from oven. Beat eggs slightly. Add sugar and beat until thick. Add lemon juice and coconut. Pour on baked crust. Bake 30 minutes longer. Sprinkle top with powdered sugar when cool. MAKES 24 BARS.

"Why don't you come to the Mill for lunch today?" [asked Hixie]

"What's the special?" [responded Qwilleran]

"Chili. Bring your own fire extinguisher."

Firehouse Chili

---

2 pounds ground beef

2 medium onions, chopped

1 15-ounce can hot enchilada sauce

2 15-ounce cans tomato sauce

2 15½-ounce cans kidney beans, drained

8 ounces sharp cheddar cheese, grated

Tabasco sauce to taste

corn chips

Preheat oven to 350°. Cook ground beef and onion together in a large skillet. Drain. Add enchilada sauce, tomato sauce, beans, cheese, and Tabasco sauce, if desired. Stir well. Pour into baking dish and bake for 30 minutes. Serve over the corn chips. SERVES 6.

He [Qwilleran] *took a handful of* **hazelnut jumbles** *and went looking for the Siamese . . . He made it a point to say good-bye to them whenever he left the house for a few hours . . . He had to dress for dinner at Polly Duncan's cottage on MacGregor Road.* *Roast beef and Yorkshire pudding!*

Hazelnut Jumbles

¾   cup butter
½   cup shortening
1½   cups powdered sugar
2½   cups all-purpose flour
½   teaspoon salt
1   cup chopped hazelnuts
2   teaspoons vanilla extract

Cream butter and shortening with an electric mixer until smooth. Beat in powdered sugar gradually. Add flour and salt. Mix well. Add hazelnuts and vanilla extract. Dough will be crumbly. Transfer dough to a piece of waxed paper. Shape to form a log approximately 12 inches long. Roll waxed paper tightly around log and refrigerate 1 hour. Cut into ½-inch slices. Bake on an ungreased cookie sheet at 325° for 15–20 minutes or until cookies are a delicate light brown. MAKES 2 DOZEN.

Roast Beef and Yorkshire Pudding

Roast beef:
- 1   4-pound rolled rib roast
- salt, pepper, and garlic powder to taste

Yorkshire pudding:
- 3   eggs
- 1   cup all-purpose flour
- ½   teaspoon salt
- 1   cup milk (approximate)
- 3   tablespoons beef drippings (approximate)

Preheat oven to 325°. Season the roast with salt, pepper, and garlic powder. Bake until meat reaches desired degree of doneness. (Meat is cooked rare when temperature reaches 120° on meat thermometer inserted into center of roast.) Then increase oven temperature to 375°. Place 2 eggs into a mixing bowl. Using an electric mixer, beat well. Add flour and salt slowly, beating the entire time. Add the last egg and beat 20 seconds. Add enough milk to make a batter of thin consistency. Beat 1 minute. Pour beef drippings into 8-inch round pan. Place pan into oven until very hot. Pour the batter onto the drippings. Bake 35–40 minutes. Serve at once with roast. SERVES 4–6.

"Did you sleep well?" she [Polly] *asked.*

"Very well." [answered Qwilleran] *"And not because of tramping through the snow or eating too much roast beef . . . I smell something good."*

"Coffee," she said, *"and scones in the oven."*

The scones were dotted with currants and served with cream cheese and gooseberry jam.

Currant Scones

2 cups all-purpose flour
1½ teaspoons cream of tartar
¾ teaspoon baking soda
⅛ teaspoon salt
1 stick butter or margarine, softened
1 egg, beaten
½ cup currants
½ cup buttermilk
1 tablespoon cream
1 tablespoon sugar
cream cheese
jam

Preheat oven to 400°. Sift or mix the flour, cream of tartar, baking soda, and salt together. Cut in the butter or margarine until the mixture is about the size of small peas. Add the egg, the currants, and enough of the buttermilk to make a soft dough. Turn out on floured surface and knead gently 4 or 5 times. Roll out ½-inch thick and cut into rounds 3 inches in diameter using a biscuit cutter or a drinking glass. Brush the tops with cream and sprinkle with sugar. Bake 12 minutes or until lightly browned on greased cookie sheet. MAKES 12. SERVE WITH CREAM CHEESE AND JAM.

NOTE: Raisins may be substituted for currants.

The Cat Who Sniffed Glue

Qwilleran loves to eat all the great foods Mrs. Cobb prepares, but Koko suddenly has an appetite for, of all things, glue! Could he be trying to give Qwill a clue to the murderer of the rich banker and his wife?

Hotel Booze Specialties

No-Holds-Barred Hamburger aka Boozeburger

Strawberry Pie

Qwilleran had three reasons for driving to the Hotel Booze in Brrr on Thursday evening. He had a yen for one of their no-holds-barred hamburgers . . .

Thelma had always served the toppling burgers with her thumb on top of the bun; now they were skewered with cocktail picks . . .

The waitress in the miniskirt announced the pie of the day: strawberry. It proved to be made with whole berries and real whipped cream, and Qwilleran and his guest [Mildred] devoured it in enraptured silence.

No-Holds-Barred Hamburger aka Boozeburger

2 pounds ground beef
½ cup beer
½ cup fine dry bread crumbs
1 teaspoon seasoned salt
¼ teaspoon pepper
½ cup finely chopped onion
8 slices bacon, cut in half
4 large buns
mayonnaise
4 slices cheddar cheese
4 thin slices onion
4 thin slices tomato
8 thin slices dill pickle
mustard
ketchup
lettuce

Mix the beef, beer, bread crumbs, salt, pepper, and onion. Shape into 8 thin patties. Fry or grill to desired degree of doneness. In separate pan, fry the bacon. To assemble, place in the following order on bottom of bun: mayonnaise, 1 burger, 1 slice cheese, a second burger, 4 half-slices bacon, slice of onion, slice of tomato, 2 slices dill pickle, mustard, ketchup, lettuce, top of bun. Insert wooden skewers. SERVES 4.

Strawberry Pie

Pastry:
- ½   cup shortening
- 1½   cups all-purpose flour
- ½   teaspoon salt
- 3–4   tablespoons ice water

Preheat oven to 425°. Cut the shortening into the flour and salt until the mixture is the size of small peas. Add the water a tablespoonful at a time, mixing lightly with a fork. When mixture holds together, gently form a ball and then roll it out on a floured surface to about ¼ inch in thickness. Place in 9-inch pie pan. Prick bottom and sides of dough with fork. Place pie weights or another lightweight pie pan on crust to keep it from bubbling up while baking. Bake 15–20 minutes or until browned.

Strawberry filling:
- 4–5   cups fresh strawberries
- 1   cup water
- 1   cup sugar
- 3   tablespoons cornstarch
- 1   cup sweetened whipped cream or whipped topping

Crush 1 cup of the strawberries. Add the water. Bring to a boil. Reduce heat and simmer for 3 minutes. Strain the juice from the cooked berries. Add enough water to make 1 cup berry juice.

Set aside. Put sugar and cornstarch in a saucepan. Slowly add berry juice to the sugar and cornstarch. Stir until smooth. Bring to a boil over medium heat, stirring constantly. Cook until thick and clear. Cool slightly. Arrange remaining berries in baked pie shell. Pour glaze over berries. Chill. Serve with whipped cream or whipped topping. SERVES 6.

À La Carte

"How did you guys know it's my birthday?" [asked Qwilleran]

Fran said, "Dad ran a check on your driver's registration."

Then someone produced paper plates and cups, and someone else unveiled a sheet cake decorated with a bugle and the theater's traditional wish: "Break a leg, darling!"

Qwilleran's Birthday Cake

½   cup butter or margarine
2   cups sugar
3½   cups all-purpose flour
1   tablespoon baking powder
1   teaspoon salt
1½   cups ice water
1½   teaspoons vanilla extract
4   egg whites

Preheat oven to 350°. Cream butter or margarine and sugar together. Sift or mix flour, baking powder, and salt thoroughly. Then add the flour mixture to the sugar mixture alternating with the water. Add the vanilla extract. Beat egg whites until stiff; gently fold into batter. Bake in a greased 9-inch by 13-inch pan about 40 minutes or until the cake pulls away from the sides of the pan. SERVES 12–14.

Frosting:
- ½   cup butter or margarine, room temperature
- ½   cup cream cheese, room temperature
- 2   teaspoons vanilla extract
- 4½ cups powdered sugar
- 3–5 tablespoons milk
- cake decorations

With an electric mixer, beat butter or margarine, cream cheese, and vanilla extract for 30 seconds. Slowly add half the powdered sugar. Add 1–2 tablespoons of the milk. Beat in rest of sugar and enough milk to make the mixture of spreading consistency. Use yellow candy-coated chocolate pieces to form the shape of a bugle on top of cake or tint part of the frosting yellow and pipe a decoration with a pastry bag.

"They [Quill and Polly] consulted the menu. It was no-frills cuisine at Tipsy's, but the cooks knew what they were doing. Polly was happy that her **pickerel** *tasted like fish and not like seasoned bread crumbs. Qwilleran was happy that his steak required chewing. "I always suspect beef that melts in my mouth," he said.*

Pickerel

---

2 pounds pickerel fillets
salt and pepper to taste
2 eggs, well beaten (optional)
2 tablespoons milk (optional)
½ cup fine dry plain bread crumbs or flour (optional)
oil
butter or margarine
2 tablespoons chopped fresh parsley
lemon wedges

Rinse fish and dry with paper towels. Cut into serving-sized pieces. Season with salt and pepper. If breaded fish are desired, mix the eggs and milk. Dip fish in egg mixture and then in bread crumbs or flour. Heat equal parts of oil and butter or margarine in skillet. Fry the fish until browned on each side—about 4 minutes. Sprinkle with parsley. Serve with lemon wedges. SERVES 4.

*Polly declined dessert, but he [Quilleran] was unable to resist the **lemon meringue pie**.*

Lemon Meringue Pie

Pastry:

- ½ cup shortening
- 1½ cups all-purpose flour
- ½ teaspoon salt
- 3–4 tablespoons ice water

Preheat oven to 425°. Cut the shortening into the flour and salt until the mixture is the size of small peas. Add the water a tablespoonful at a time, mixing lightly with a fork. When mixture holds together, gently form a ball and then roll it out on a floured surface to about ¼ inch in thickness. Place in 9-inch pie pan. Prick bottom and sides of dough with fork. Place pie weights or another lightweight pie pan on crust to keep it from bubbling up while baking. Bake 15–20 minutes or until browned.

Lemon filling:

- 1½ cups sugar
- ¼ cup cornstarch
- 3 tablespoons all-purpose flour
- 1½ cups water
- 3 egg yolks, beaten slightly (reserve whites)
- 3 tablespoons butter or margarine
- ⅓ cup lemon juice
- 1 tablespoon grated lemon rind

Preheat oven to 375°. Mix sugar, cornstarch, and flour in a saucepan. Stir in water gradually. Cook over medium heat, stirring constantly until mixture is thick. Boil for one minute. Very slowly, so as not to cook the yolks, stir about half the mixture into the egg yolks. Then blend the yolk mixture back into the original hot mixture. Boil for another minute, stirring constantly. Remove from heat and stir until smooth. Add the butter or margarine, lemon juice, and grated rind. Pour into baked crust. Let cool slightly. Cover with meringue (see recipe below), making sure the meringue touches the inside of the crust all the way around to prevent shrinkage. Bake about 12 minutes or until meringue turns a light brown. SERVES 6.

Meringue:

- 1 tablespoon cornstarch
- 2 tablespoons cold water
- ½ cup water
- 3 egg whites
- 6 tablespoons sugar
- 1 teaspoon lemon juice

Blend cornstarch with 2 tablespoons cold water. Bring ½ cup water to a boil in a small saucepan. Stir cornstarch mixture into the boiling water. Cook until thick. Place saucepan in cold water. Set aside. Beat egg whites until they form soft peaks. Add sugar slowly and beat until glossy. Add cooled cornstarch mixture and lemon juice to egg whites all at once. Blend well.

"Let's go to dinner," Qwilleran said [to Francesca] . . .

They drove to Stephanie's, one of the best restaurants in the county...
Qwilleran always likes walking into a restaurant with Francesca. On this
occasion, heads turned to admire the young woman . . .

Perusing the menu, he suggested the ℋerbed trout with wine sauce.

"I'd rather have the spareribs,*" she said.*

"The trout is better for you."

"Will you stop sounding like my dad, Qwill?"

ℋerbed Trout with Wine Sauce

½   lemon, sliced
¼   cup chopped onion
1   teaspoon dried tarragon
¾   teaspoon + ¼ teaspoon dried basil
salt and pepper to taste
4   8-ounce trout, cleaned
2   tablespoons butter or margarine
2   tablespoons all-purpose flour
½   cup half-and-half
½   cup dry white wine

𝒫lace lemon slices, onion, tarragon, ¾ teaspoon basil, salt, and pepper on the bottom of a shallow pan. Arrange the trout over the lemon, onion, and seasonings. Add enough water to completely cover the fish. Bring to a boil. Reduce heat, cover, and simmer about 5 minutes. Remove from pan. Place fish on a plate and cover with foil to keep warm. In a small saucepan, melt the butter or margarine and blend the flour into it. Add half-and-half slowly and cook until thick, stirring constantly. Add wine and ¼ teaspoon basil. Another ½ cup of half-and-half can be substituted for the wine, if desired. Continue to cook if thicker sauce is desired. Pour over fish. Serve with wild rice. SERVES 4.

Spareribs

5 pounds pork spareribs
salt and pepper to taste
¾ teaspoon dry mustard
¾ cup brown sugar, packed
3 tablespoons cornstarch
1 teaspoon ginger
¼ cup lemon juice
2 cups orange juice
¼ cup soy sauce
1 cup sliced fresh mushrooms
⅓ cup chopped onion
2 tablespoons butter or margarine
2 green peppers, cut into serving-size pieces
1 20-ounce can pineapple chunks sweetened in own juice, drained

Preheat oven to 350°. Place spareribs in baking pan or dish. Season with salt and pepper and bake, covered, 1½ hours or until meat is nearly tender. Pour off fat. Leave ribs in baking pan. Combine dry mustard, sugar, cornstarch, and ginger in a saucepan. Add lemon juice, orange juice, and soy sauce. Cook until thickened, stirring constantly. Pour sauce over ribs. Sauté the mushrooms and onion in the butter or margarine. Then place mushrooms, onion, green peppers, and pineapple in the pan with the ribs. Cover and bake 25–30 minutes. Baste with the sauce several times. Serve with rice. SERVES 4.

"Would you like a cup of coffee or a cold drink or beer?" Qwilleran asked.

"I wouldn't mind something to drink. Coffee, I guess. Gotta stay sober on this job, even if it isn't all stripes." [said Pete the paper-hanger]

Qwilleran thawed some frozen coffee cake in the microwave, pressed buttons on the computerized coffee maker, and served the repast in the studio, among the ladders and paste buckets.

Coffee Cake

¾ cup butter or margarine
1½ cups sugar
4 eggs
3 cups + 2 tablespoons all-purpose flour
1½ teaspoons baking powder
1½ teaspoons baking soda
1 pint sour cream
2 teaspoons vanilla extract
½ cup chopped pecans
½ cup brown sugar, packed
1 teaspoon cinnamon

Preheat oven to 350°. Cream butter or margarine and sugar until light and fluffy. Beat in eggs, 1 at a time. Sift or mix 3 cups of the flour, baking powder, and soda . Add dry ingredients to the egg mixture, alternating with the sour cream. Add vanilla extract. To make filling, mix the pecans, brown sugar, remaining 2 tablespoons flour, and cinnamon. Alternate layers of batter and filling in a greased tube pan, beginning and ending with the batter. Bake for 1 hour and 10 minutes. Let stand about 15 minutes before removing from the pan. MAKES 15–20 SLICES.

After the work was finished and Pete had cleared out his ladders and buckets, it was late. Qwilleran had no desire to go out to a restaurant, so he thawed some frozen stew for himself and gave the cats the rest of their chicken liver pâté.

Beef Stew

2 pounds stew meat
¼ cup all-purpose flour
½ teaspoon salt
¼ teaspoon pepper
¼ cup butter or margarine
3 cups water
1 10½-ounce can beef broth
1 onion, chopped
1 clove garlic, chopped
2 4-ounce cans mushrooms or ½ pound sliced fresh mushrooms
1 stalk celery, sliced
6 carrots, sliced
6 potatoes, diced

*P*ut the stew meat, flour, salt, and pepper in a bag and shake to coat the meat. Brown the meat in the butter or margarine in a large saucepan. Add water, beef broth, onion, and garlic. Simmer, covered, 40–45 minutes. Add the mushrooms, celery, carrots, and potatoes. Simmer, covered, until meat and vegetables are tender. Thicken with additional flour, if desired. Serves 6.

The Cat Who Went Underground

Qwilleran, Koko, and Yum Yum think they're going to have a relaxing summer at their log cabin. Then dead bodies start turning up. Is it murder? Will the trio be able to solve the crimes?

Wimsey Family Reunion Fare

Fried Chicken

Baked Beans

Cornish Pasties

Ham Sandwiches

Deviled Eggs

Reunion Potato Salad

Homemade Freezer Pickles

Apple Juice Salad

Granny Wimsey's Chocolate Sheet Cake

Thimbleberry Pie

Molasses Cookies

❖

"I was considering a column on family reunions. Are they closed sessions, or could a reporter barge in?" [asked Qwilleran]

"They'd be thrilled to have someone from the newspaper! They really would!" [answered Mildred]

"There was an announcement in the paper that the Wimsey family is having a reunion this Sunday on someone's farm." [said Qwilleran]

Long rows of picnic tables were set up, and families arrived with hampers, coolers, and folding lawn chairs . . .

The long tables were loaded with fried chicken, baked beans, and Cornish pasties; ham sandwiches, deviled eggs, potato salad, homemade pickles . . . berry pies and molasses cookies.

Fried Chicken

1   3-pound broiler-fryer, cut up
1   cup buttermilk
1   cup all-purpose flour
1   teaspoon salt
½   teaspoon black pepper
½   teaspoon paprika
oil

Place chicken in a shallow baking dish. Pour buttermilk over chicken. Cover and refrigerate 2 hours. Turn once in buttermilk while refrigerated. Put flour, salt, pepper, and paprika in a large plastic bag. Remove chicken from buttermilk and place in flour mixture a few pieces at a time.

Shake to coat. Heat oil to 350° in a large frying pan. Fry chicken until browned, turning once. Lower heat to 275°. Cover pan and cook 25–30 minutes. Drain on paper towels. SERVES 4.

Baked Beans

---

2   16-ounce cans pork and beans
½   cup brown sugar, packed
½   cup chopped onion
1   tablespoon prepared mustard
¼   cup ketchup
uncooked bacon strips

Preheat oven to 350°. Mix beans, sugar, onion, mustard, and ketchup. Put into baking dish. Place bacon over the top. Bake 30–45 minutes. SERVES 4–6.

Cornish Pasties

Pastry:
1½   cups lard
4   cups flour
2   teaspoons salt
8–10   tablespoons water

Cut lard into flour and salt with pastry blender or fork. Add water a little at a time, mixing lightly with fork. When dough clings together, form into ball. Divide ball of dough into 2 sections.

Filling:

- ⅔ cup lean ground beef
- ⅔ cup finely chopped turnips
- ⅔ cup finely chopped onion
- ⅔ cup finely chopped potatoes
- ¾ teaspoon salt
- ½ teaspoon pepper
- 1 egg, beaten

Preheat oven to 375°. Mix beef, turnips, onion, potatoes, salt, and pepper thoroughly. Roll out 1 ball of pastry to ¼ inch in thickness. Cut into 6-inch circles. Place a tablespoon of filling on half of each circle. Moisten the top edge of the dough with water. Fold top of dough down over meat filling and crimp with tines of fork. Make several small slashes in pasty to allow steam to escape. Brush top with egg. Repeat procedure with second ball of dough. Bake 40 minutes on ungreased cookie sheet. MAKES 10–12 PASTIES.

Ham Sandwiches

- ¼ cup butter or margarine, room temperature
- 3 tablespoons Dijon mustard
- 3 tablespoons finely chopped mild onion
- 1 teaspoon ground horseradish
- 2 teaspoons poppy seeds
- 8 hamburger buns
- 8 slices baked or boiled ham
- 8 slices Swiss cheese

Preheat oven to 350°. Mix butter, mustard, onion, horseradish, and poppy seeds thoroughly. Slice buns, if necessary, and spread mixture on both sides of each bun. Put a slice of ham and a slice of cheese on the bottom of each bun. Place bun top over cheese; wrap in foil. Bake 20–25 minutes. MAKES 8 SANDWICHES.

Deviled Eggs

6 hard-boiled eggs
¼ teaspoon salt
⅛ teaspoon pepper
¼ cup mayonnaise
¼ cup sweet pickle relish
paprika

Carefully remove shells from eggs. Cut in half lengthwise. Remove egg yolks. Combine yolks with salt, pepper, and mayonnaise. Mix until smooth. Add pickle relish. Do not drain the relish if a creamier yolk is desired. Place in cooked egg whites. Sprinkle with paprika. SERVES 6.

Reunion Potato Salad

4 cups peeled and cubed potatoes
1 teaspoon salt
¼ cup finely chopped onion
¼ cup finely chopped celery
¼ cup finely chopped carrots
½ cup mayonnaise or salad dressing
¼ cup sour cream
1 teaspoon prepared mustard
2 tablespoons ketchup
salt and pepper to taste
2 hard-boiled eggs, chopped

Place potatoes in saucepan. Cover with water; add salt. Boil potatoes until tender. Drain. To make dressing, stir together onion, celery, carrots, mayonnaise or salad dressing, sour cream, mustard, ketchup, additional salt, if desired, and pepper. Gently add warm potatoes and eggs to the dressing. Chill. SERVES 4–6.

Homemade Freezer Pickles

2 cups sugar

1 cup white vinegar

7 cups sliced pickling cucumbers (¼-inch thick), not peeled

1 green or red sweet pepper, cut into strips

1 cup sliced onion

1½ tablespoons salt

½ tablespoon celery salt

1 tablespoon celery seed

Put the sugar and vinegar in a saucepan and bring to a boil. Stir until the sugar is dissolved. Remove from the heat. Put the cucumbers, pepper, onion, salt, celery salt, and celery seed into a bowl and mix. Pour the vinegar mixture over the cucumber mixture. Place into smaller containers and freeze. Thaw in the refrigerator before serving. SERVES 10–12.

Apple Juice Salad

1 3-ounce package lemon gelatin

2 cups hot apple juice

1 tablespoon lemon juice

1 cup unpeeled, diced apples

½ cup pecans, coarsely chopped

½ cup finely chopped celery

Dissolve gelatin in apple juice. Add lemon juice. Chill until gelatin begins to thicken. Fold in the apples, pecans, and celery. Pour into 1-quart mold. Chill. SERVES 4.

Granny Wimsey's Chocolate Sheet Cake

2   cups sugar
2   cups all-purpose flour
½   cup butter or margarine
½   cup shortening
2½   tablespoons cocoa
1   cup water
½   cup buttermilk
2   eggs, beaten slightly
1   teaspoon baking soda
1   teaspoon cinnamon
1   teaspoon vanilla extract

Preheat oven to 400°. Sift sugar and flour together. Place butter or margarine, shortening, cocoa, and water in saucepan; bring to a boil and pour over flour mixture. Mix well. Stir in buttermilk and eggs. Add baking soda, cinnamon, and vanilla extract; stir. Pour into a greased 9-inch by 13-inch pan. Bake for 20 minutes.

Frosting:
½   cup butter or margarine
2½   tablespoons cocoa
6   tablespoons milk
1   1-pound box powdered sugar
1   teaspoon vanilla extract
2   cups chopped pecans

In a saucepan, mix butter or margarine, cocoa, and milk. Bring to a boil and remove from heat. Add powdered sugar and vanilla extract. Mix well. Add pecans. Spread warm frosting on warm cake.

Thimbleberry Pie

Pastry:
- ½ cup shortening
- 1½ cups all-purpose flour
- ½ teaspoon salt
- 3–4 tablespoons ice water

Preheat oven to 400°. Cut the shortening into the flour and salt until the mixture is the size of small peas. Add the water a tablespoonful at a time, mixing lightly with a fork. When mixture holds together, gently form into a ball. Roll out into a circle about ¼ inch in thickness. Place in 9-inch pie pan. Prick bottom and sides of dough with fork. Place pie weights or another lightweight pie pan over crust to keep it from bubbling up while baking. Bake 15–20 minutes or until browned.

Berry filling:
- 4 cups raspberries or blackberries
- 1 cup water
- ½ cup + ¼ cup sugar
- 2 tablespoons cornstarch
- 1 tablespoon butter or margarine
- ½ teaspoon lemon juice
- pinch of salt
- 1 cup whipping cream
- ¼ cup powdered sugar
- ½ teaspoon vanilla extract

Put 1 cup of the raspberries or blackberries, the water, and ½ cup of the sugar in a saucepan. Simmer and stir for 2 to 3 minutes or until sugar is dissolved. Press through a sieve to remove seeds. Add water, if necessary, to make 1 cup of berry juice. Dissolve cornstarch in ¼ cup of the juice. Then mix with the rest of the juice. Bring to a boil and cook, stirring, until thickened—about 5 minutes. Remove from the heat and stir in the butter or margarine, the remaining ¼ cup sugar, lemon juice, and salt. Put half the remaining berries in the baked piecrust and top with half the cooked mixture. Then add the rest of the berries and the remaining cooked mixture. Chill. Serve topped with whipped cream mixed with powdered sugar and vanilla extract or use whipped topping. SERVES 6.

NOTE: Any thimble-shaped fruit, such as raspberries or blackberries, is considered to be a thimbleberry and can be used in this recipe.

Molasses Cookies

1 cup sugar
1 cup shortening, melted
1 cup molasses
1 egg, beaten
4 cups all-purpose flour
½ teaspoon salt
1 teaspoon baking soda
1 teaspoon cinnamon
1 teaspoon ginger
1 cup boiling water

Preheat oven to 350°. Mix sugar and melted shortening. Add the molasses and egg. Sift or mix the dry ingredients and stir them into the molasses mixture. Add the water and mix well. Let stand an hour and then drop by heaping teaspoonsful onto greased cookie sheets. Bake 10–15 minutes. Let stand on cookie sheet for several minutes before removing to cooling racks. MAKES ABOUT 5 DOZEN COOKIES.

À La Carte

"Why don't you come over here for dinner tonight? I'll throw together a casserole and a salad and take a pie out of the freezer." [asked Mildred]

Qwilleran accepted promptly. . . .

The casserole was a sauced combination of turkey, homemade noodles, and artichoke hearts, and it put Qwilleran in an excellent frame of mind.

Turkey Noodle Casserole

Homemade noodles:

- 1 egg
- 1 tablespoon milk
- ½ teaspoon + 1 teaspoon oil
- ½ teaspoon + 1 teaspoon salt
- ¾ cup all-purpose flour (approximately)

Mix egg, milk, ½ teaspoon oil, and ½ teaspoon salt in medium-sized bowl. Add enough flour to make a stiff dough. Cover bowl and let dough rest 15 minutes. Roll out on floured board into a rectangle about ⅛-inch in thickness and approximately 15-inches by 13-inches. Let stand 15 minutes before rolling into a tube about 15-inches long. Cut into 1-inch sections. Unroll noodles and allow to dry for 30 minutes. Drop into large pan of boiling water to which 1 teaspoon oil and 1 teaspoon salt has been added. Boil about 8 minutes. Drain.

NOTE: 1 8-ounce package cooked lasagne noodles can be substituted for homemade noodles.

Turkey mixture:

1   10¾-ounce can cream of mushroom soup
⅔   cup milk
½   teaspoon salt
¼   teaspoon pepper
½   teaspoon poultry seasoning
1   8-ounce package cream cheese, room temperature
1   cup cottage cheese
½   cup chopped onion
⅓   cup chopped green pepper
5   fresh artichoke hearts, cooked, quartered or 1 14-ounce can artichoke hearts, quartered
3   cups diced cooked turkey
1½   cups bread crumbs
¼   cup melted butter or margarine

Preheat oven to 375°. Combine and then heat soup, milk, salt, pepper, and poultry seasoning. Mix cream cheese and cottage cheese in a separate bowl. Stir the onion and green pepper into the cheese mixture; then fold in artichoke hearts and turkey. Place half the noodles in a baking dish or pan approximately 9-inches by 13-inches in size. Spread with half the cheese mixture and half the soup mixture. Repeat. Top with bread crumbs. Drizzle with melted butter or margarine. Bake 30 minutes. SERVES 6–8.

The raspberry pie left him almost numb with contentment.

Raspberry Pie

1   8-ounce carton whipped topping, thawed
2   8-ounce cartons raspberry yogurt
1   10-ounce package frozen raspberries in syrup, thawed, mashed
½   cup powdered sugar
1   commercially prepared deep-dish graham-cracker crust
chocolate syrup

Mix whipped topping and yogurt. Fold in raspberries and powdered sugar. Pour into pie shell and freeze several hours or overnight. Thaw slightly and drizzle with chocolate syrup before serving. SERVES 6.

He [Qwilleran] telephoned Arch Riker. "Are you free for dinner tonight, Arch? It's been a long time."

"Sure has!" said Riker. Because of his approaching marriage and the pressures of launching a new publication he had not been available for bachelor dinners for many weeks. "I'm free, and I'm hungry. What did you have in mind?"

"I've moved up to the cabin for the summer. Why don't you meet me there, and we'll go to the Northern Lights Hotel. They have spaghetti on Mondays . . ."

The salad was crisp, the garlic bread was crusty, and the spaghetti was al dente. "It's the best thing they do," Qwilleran said.

Spaghetti

1   pound ground beef
1   6-ounce can tomato paste
1   8-ounce can tomato sauce
1   14½-ounce can diced tomatoes
1   onion, chopped
½   green pepper, chopped
1   clove garlic, chopped
1   4-ounce can mushrooms, drained
1   cup water
½–1   teaspoon Italian seasoning
salt and pepper to taste
1   pound of spaghetti

Cook ground beef in a large skillet, stirring to crumble it into very small pieces; drain fat. Add remaining ingredients except the spaghetti. Simmer for about an hour. Boil spaghetti to al dente stage. Serve with sauce. SERVES 4–6.

Garlic Bread

———

2   cloves garlic, minced
¼   cup butter or margarine
4   ounces cream cheese, softened
1   loaf Italian bread, split lengthwise

Preheat oven to 425°. Sauté garlic in butter or margarine. Mix garlic and butter or margarine with the cream cheese. Spread bread liberally with mixture. Wrap in aluminum foil. Bake 15 minutes. For crusty bread, remove foil the last 5 minutes. SERVES 4–6.

"How do you feel about living up here? Have you adjusted?" [asked Qwilleran]

*Riker gave his **martini** a trial sip, winced, and nodded approval. "Yes, I'm glad to be here."*

Martini

———

ice cubes
2½   ounces dry gin
½   ounce dry vermouth
olive

Place ice in glass and add gin, then vermouth. Stir gently. Strain to remove ice. SERVE IN A 3-OUNCE GLASS WITH AN OLIVE.

[Cecil Huggins said] *"My grandfather used to have a general store . . . There was an old geezer who used to come in to swipe crackers out of the barrel . . . Josh Cummins, his name was. And on his way out of the store after a game of checkers with his cronies around the stove, he'd always pick up a loaf of bread—the one nearest the door—and never pay for it. It griped Grandpa more and more every time . . . so he thought of a scheme. He told Grandma to bake a* loaf of bread *with a dirty sock in it . . . The old guy picked it up and walked out . . . Never stole another loaf!"*

"Dirty Sock" Bread

1   package dry yeast
2   cups lukewarm milk (105–115°)
3   tablespoons shortening
2   teaspoons salt
3   teaspoons sugar
4–5   cups all-purpose flour
melted shortening for top of dough
1   "dirty sock" (optional)

Preheat oven to 375°. Dissolve the yeast in ½ cup of the milk. In a large bowl, mix the shortening, salt, sugar, and remaining milk. Let mixture cool. Beat in about 2 cups of the flour. Add the yeast mixture. Then add enough of the remaining flour to make a soft dough. Dough may be sticky. Place dough in a greased bowl and brush the top with a little melted shortening. Cover and let rise until doubled in size, about 1 hour. Shape into 2 loaves. (Grandma added a dirty sock at this point.) Place into greased bread pans. Cover and let rise until doubled in size again, about 45 minutes. Bake at 375° about 30 minutes. SERVES 6.

*"How's the **pie**?" asked the proprietor, making his rounds.*

"Best I ever tasted, Gary," said Qwilleran. "Is your grandmother still making your pies?"

"No, the old lady died, but my aunt has her recipes."

"It's rich but not cloying, creamy but not viscid."

"I should raise the price," Gary said as he walked away to ring up a sale on the antique brass cash register.

Best Ever Chocolate Meringue Pie

Pastry:
- ½ cup shortening
- 1 cup all-purpose flour
- ¼ teaspoon salt
- ¼ cup finely chopped pecans
- 2–3 tablespoons water

Preheat oven to 350°. Cut shortening into flour using pastry blender or 2 knives until pastry is the consistency of very coarse cornmeal. Mix in salt and pecans. Add water a tablespoonful at a time. Mix lightly until dough holds together. Roll dough to approximately ¼ inch in thickness on floured surface. Place in 8-inch pie pan. Place pie weights or another lightweight pan on top while baking to prevent bubbles from forming. Bake 15–20 minutes.

Pie filling:

- 4 tablespoons cocoa
- 3 tablespoons cornstarch
- 6 tablespoons + 4 tablespoons sugar
- ¼ teaspoon salt
- 2 eggs, separated
- 2 cups milk
- 1 teaspoon vanilla extract

Sift cocoa or mash any lumps with the back of a spoon. Sift or mix cornstarch, cocoa, 6 tablespoons of the sugar, and salt together. Place the mixture in the top of a double boiler. Beat the egg yolks slightly. While stirring the cocoa mixture, add the milk slowly, and then the egg yolks. Cook over medium heat, stirring constantly until mixture is thick. Add vanilla extract. Cool slightly. Put mixture in cooled pecan piecrust or baked commercially prepared crust. Beat egg whites, gradually adding 4 tablespoons sugar until soft peaks form. Spread on pie. Brown under broiler. SERVES 6.

The Cat Who Talked to Ghosts

Qwilleran's favorite cook, Mrs. Cobb, was hearing noises in the farmhouse where she was living. She called Qwill, but he was too late to help her. Now it's up to Qwill and Koko to solve the mystery of her death.

Northern Lights Hotel Supper

French Onion Soup

🐾

Broiled Whitefish

🐾

Petite Salad

🐾

Frog Legs

🐾

Northern Lights Hotel Pumpkin Pecan Pie

"Are you free to have dinner tonight?" [Qwilleran asked Mildred Hanstable]

"I'm always free to have dinner. That's my problem."

"I'll pick you up at six-thirty, and we'll go to the Northern Lights Hotel."

She [Mildred] glanced at the menu. "And a hundred years ago this hotel served slumgullion to deckhands and prospectors, instead of *broiled whitefish* and petite *salads* to dieters. What are you having, Qwill? You never have to worry about calories."

"Since the cats are having lobster tonight, I think I'm entitled to *French onion soup, frog legs*, Caesar salad, and *pumpkin pecan pie*." [answered Qwill]

French Onion Soup

2   tablespoons butter or margarine
2   tablespoons cooking oil
1¾   cups thinly sliced onion
¼   teaspoon sugar
3   14½-ounce cans beef broth
     salt and pepper to taste
4   thick slices French bread, toasted
1   cup Gruyère cheese, shredded

Heat butter or margarine and oil in saucepan. Add onion slices and sugar. Cook about 20 minutes, stirring occasionally, until the onions are golden brown. Add broth and bring to a boil. Simmer 20 minutes. Add salt and pepper. Put soup into 4 bowls and top with toasted bread. Sprinkle cheese on toast. Broil until cheese melts. SERVES 4.

Broiled Whitefish

¼ cup butter or margarine
⅛ cup olive oil
1 tablespoon fresh lemon juice
½ teaspoon dried tarragon
½ teaspoon dried basil
1½ pounds whitefish

To make herb sauce, melt butter or margarine in a saucepan. Add the olive oil, lemon juice, tarragon, and basil. Remove from heat. Let sit for several minutes to release the flavor of the herbs. Preheat the broiler. Grease pan to prevent the fish from sticking. Place the fish 4 to 6 inches from the heat, depending on the thickness of the fish. Grill until the fish is opaque. Fish does not require turning unless it is more than an inch-and-a-half thick. Spoon desired amount of herb sauce over the fish before serving. SERVES 2–3.

Petite Salad

½ cup vegetable oil
⅓ cup cider vinegar
4 teaspoons sugar or equivalent amount of sugar substitute
2 teaspoons dried tarragon
1 teaspoon salt
½ teaspoon black pepper
salad greens

Blend in a blender or whisk together the oil, vinegar, sugar or sugar substitute, tarragon, salt, and pepper until sugar is dissolved and dressing is creamy. Serve over salad greens of choice. SERVES 4.

Frog Legs

10 frog legs
1 tablespoon milk
2 eggs, beaten
cracker crumbs, finely crushed
oil and butter or margarine for frying—¼ cup each (approximate)
1 onion, sliced

Skin the frog legs and remove feet. Rinse and pat dry. Add the milk to the eggs. Dip the skinned frog legs into the egg mixture and then into the cracker crumbs. Heat butter or margarine and oil in a skillet. Add the frog legs and onion. Pan fry until frog legs are golden brown—about 3 minutes on each side. Serve with onions. SERVES 6.

Northern Lights Hotel Pumpkin Pecan Pie

Pastry:
½ cup shortening
1½ cups flour
½ teaspoon salt
3–4 tablespoons ice water

Cut the shortening into the flour and salt until the mixture is the size of small peas. Add the water a tablespoonful at a time, mixing lightly with a fork. Add just enough water to hold the pastry together. Roll out on a floured surface to ¼ inch in thickness. Place in a 9-inch pie pan.

Pumpkin pecan filling:

- ¼ cup brown sugar, packed
- ½ cup sugar
- 1½ teaspoons pumpkin pie spice
- ½ teaspoon salt
- 1 15-ounce can pumpkin
- 1 12-ounce can evaporated milk
- 2 eggs, beaten slightly
- 2 tablespoons butter or margarine
- ¼ cup brown sugar
- ½ cup pecans, chopped

Preheat oven to 450°. In a saucepan, mix sugars, spice and salt. Add pumpkin and evaporated milk. Heat, stirring, to the boiling point. Remove from heat. Stir a small amount of the pumpkin mixture into the beaten eggs. Then gradually stir the eggs into the pumpkin mixture. Pour into unbaked pie shell. Bake at 450° for 10 minutes; reduce heat to 350°. Bake 30–35 minutes longer. Melt the butter or margarine. Add the brown sugar and pecans. Stir until blended and remove from heat. Sprinkle pecan mixture over the pie and bake 3 minutes longer. SERVES 6.

À La Carte

The freezer-chest contained, Qwilleran estimated, a two-month supply of spaghetti sauce, chili, macaroni and cheese (his favorite), vichyssoise, pot roast, **turkey tetrazzini,** *shrimp gumbo, deviled crab, Swedish meatballs, and other Cobb specialties—nothing in curry sauce, he was glad to note.*

Turkey Tetrazzini

1	6-ounce package medium-sized noodles
6	tablespoons butter or margarine
6	tablespoons all-purpose flour
1	10½-ounce can chicken broth
⅔	cup water
1	cup half-and-half
1	4½-ounce jar mushrooms, drained
½	cup slivered almonds
2	cups bite-sized pieces cooked turkey
	salt and pepper to taste
½	cup cheddar cheese, shredded

Preheat oven to 350°. Cook noodles in boiling water until tender. Drain. In a large skillet, over medium heat, melt the butter or margarine, add the flour and blend. Add broth and water. Cook until thickened, stirring constantly. Remove from heat. Scald half-and-half; stir slowly into broth mixture. Add mushrooms, almonds and turkey. Season with salt and pepper. Mix noodles and turkey mixture gently. Place in a greased baking dish. Top with cheese. Bake, uncovered, for about 40 minutes. SERVES 4–6.

"Would you like a glass of wine?" [asked Kristi]

"Thanks, Ms. Waffle, but alcohol isn't on my list of vices." [answered Qwilleran]

"Then how about some fresh lemonade made with honey from local bees?"

"Now you're speaking my language."

Fresh Lemonade

1   lemon, juiced
2   tablespoons honey
crushed ice
water

Place lemon juice and honey into 8-ounce glass. Add crushed ice. Stir while adding water.

Tipsy's was a popular restaurant in North Kennebeck that had started in a small log cabin in the 1930s and now occupied a large log cabin, where serious eaters converged for serious steaks without such frivolities as parsley sprigs and herbed butter. Potatoes were peeled and Frenched in the kitchen without benefit of sodium acid pyrophosphate. The only vegetable choice was boiled carrots. The only salad was coleslaw. And there was a waiting line for tables every night.

Tipsy's Coleslaw

3   slices bacon, cut into small pieces
2   tablespoons sugar
½   teaspoon salt
3   tablespoons vinegar
2   tablespoons finely chopped onion
2   cups shredded cabbage

Fry the bacon pieces and drain on paper towel. Over medium-high heat, stir sugar, salt, and vinegar into bacon drippings until mixture boils for 1 minute. Mix the bacon, onion, and cabbage. Pour the hot mixture over the cabbage mixture. Mix well. Serve immediately. SERVES 4.

Qwilleran remained and ordered Tipsy's old-fashioned bread pudding with a pitcher of thick cream for pouring, followed by two cups of coffee powerful enough to exorcise demons and domesticate poltergeists.

Tipsy's Old-Fashioned Bread Pudding

4   cups of ½-inch square bread cubes
½   cup raisins
2   cups milk, scalded, and cooled slightly
¼   cup butter, melted
½   cup sugar
2   eggs, beaten
¼   teaspoon salt
½   teaspoon cinnamon or nutmeg

Preheat oven to 350°. Put bread squares into 1½ quart buttered baking dish. Sprinkle with raisins. Mix together the milk, butter, sugar, eggs, salt, and spice. Pour over bread cubes. Put the baking dish into a pan of hot water and bake about 45 minutes until toothpick inserted in center comes out clean. Serve with cream. SERVES 4.

Next Qwilleran phoned Polly at the library. He said, "I'm driving into Pickax to do errands. Would you care to join me there for dinner?"

"Delighted," she said, "provided it's early. I must go home, you know, to feed my little sweetheart." [kitten]

"Why don't you come to my apartment when the library closes?" he suggested. "I'll have the Old Stone Mill send over some food . . ."

*A tall lanky busboy arrived with Polly's salad and Qwilleran's **lamb chop** . . .*

Lamb Chops

4   lamb loin chops, ¾-inch thick
4   teaspoons soy sauce
½   teaspoon ground ginger
½   teaspoon garlic powder
salt and pepper to taste

Brush both sides of the lamb chops with soy sauce. Sprinkle with ground ginger and garlic powder. Season with salt and pepper. Broil, 3 inches from the heat, approximately 5 minutes on each side. SERVES 2–4.

*. . . plus two servings of **pumpkin chiffon pie** with the compliments of the chef.*

Pumpkin Chiffon Pie

Pastry:
½   cup shortening
1½   cups flour
½   teaspoon salt
3–4   tablespoons ice water

Cut the shortening into the flour and salt until the mixture is the size of small peas. Add the water a tablespoonful at a time, mixing lightly with a fork. Add just enough water to hold the pastry together. Roll out on a floured surface to ¼ inch in thickness. Place in 9-inch pie pan. Prick bottom and sides to allow air to escape while baking. Pie weights or another pie pan can be placed on crust to help ensure air bubbles do not form.

Pumpkin filling:

- 2 envelopes unflavored gelatin
- ½ cup cold water
- 3 egg yolks
- ½ cup + ½ cup sugar
- 1½ cups canned pumpkin
- ½ cup milk
- ¼ teaspoon salt
- 2 teaspoons pumpkin pie spice
- 1 cup whipping cream
- whipped cream or whipped topping for garnish (optional)

Place the gelatin in the water. In a mixing bowl, beat the egg yolks with ½ cup sugar. Add the pumpkin, milk, salt, and spice to the egg mixture. Cook in a double boiler until thick, stirring constantly. Add the gelatin. Continue to stir until the gelatin is dissolved. Cool until it begins to thicken. Beat the whipping cream and the other ½ cup sugar until stiff peaks form. Fold into the pumpkin mixture. Pour into baked pie shell. Chill. Garnish with additional whipped cream or whipped topping, if desired. SERVES 6–8.

The Cat Who Lived High

Quilleran wants to save the historic Casablanca apartment building from demolition and help with the restoration. When he, Koko, and Yum Yum move into the penthouse apartment to be closer to the project, they discover that an art dealer was killed in the very apartment in which they are living.

Dinner at Courtney's Place

Cream of Watercress Soup

Courtney's Crabcakes

Shiitake Mushrooms

Glazed Beets

Wild Rice

Hearts and Sprouts Salad

Chocolate Soufflé

🐾

"Now—let me tell you about Courtney's place so it won't come as a total shock . . . He doesn't have any furniture."

. . . Courtney lighted candles at the dark end of the room, where planks were laid across columns of concrete blocks to form a long narrow table . . . The seats were upended orange crates, each with a velvet cushion weighted at the four corners with tassles . . . For a table centerpiece white carnations were arranged with weeds from the parking lot. Pewter service plates and goblets were set on the bare boards, and there were four tall pewter candlesticks.

The soup course was **cream of watercress** *. . .*

Cream of Watercress Soup

½   cup chopped onion
1   cup chopped potato
1   clove garlic, chopped
3   tablespoons butter or margarine
2   cups coarsely chopped watercress
2   tablespoons all-purpose flour
½   teaspoon salt
⅛   teaspoon pepper
1   14½-ounce can chicken broth
2   cups half-and-half

Sauté onion, potato, and garlic in butter or margarine over medium heat for 3 minutes. Add the watercress and cook 3 minutes, stirring constantly. Blend in flour, salt, and pepper; add chicken broth slowly. Stir until thickened. Continue to cook over low heat until potatoes are tender, stirring occasionally. Add half-and-half. Do not allow to boil. SERVES 4.

. . . followed by **crabcakes** *. . .*

Courtney's Crabcakes

⅓ cup finely chopped onion

2 tablespoons butter or margarine

2 eggs, beaten

⅔ cup fine dry bread crumbs

⅛ cup cream

2½ teaspoons Worcestershire sauce

1 teaspoon lemon juice

2 6-ounce cans crabmeat

½ teaspoon salt

¼ teaspoon pepper

fine dry bread crumbs for coating cakes—approximately ½ cup

cooking oil

In a small skillet sauté the onion in the butter or margarine until tender. Combine the eggs, bread crumbs, cream, Worcestershire sauce, and lemon juice in a bowl. Stir in the onion, crabmeat, salt, and pepper. Shape into cakes about ½-inch thick. If cakes are too soft, add bread crumbs. If too stiff, add cream. Coat with bread crumbs. Heat the cooking oil in a skillet. Add crabcakes and fry over medium-high heat about 2 minutes on each side or until golden brown. MAKES 4 TO 6 CAKES.

Shiitake Mushrooms

---

4   large shiitake mushrooms, washed and patted dry
½   cup all-purpose flour (approximate)
2   tablespoons butter or margarine
1   tablespoon oil

Wash and slice the mushrooms into strips. Put the flour into a small paper or plastic bag. Place the mushrooms in the bag and shake gently until coated with flour. Heat the butter or margarine and oil in a skillet. Add the mushrooms and fry about 3 minutes on each side or until golden brown. SERVES 3–4.

. . . *baby beets in an orange glaze* . . .

Glazed Beets

⅓   cup sugar
2   tablespoons cornstarch
¼   teaspoon salt
¾   cup orange juice
2   tablespoons lemon juice
1½   tablespoons butter or margarine
3½   cups canned, sliced small beets

Mix sugar, cornstarch, and salt. Stir while gradually adding orange juice and lemon juice. Cook over medium heat until thick, stirring the entire time. Add butter or margarine; continue stirring until butter or margarine melts. Place beets in a small saucepan over medium-high heat. Bring to a boil, remove from heat, drain excess liquid. Place in a serving dish and pour warm glaze over beets. SERVES 4–6.

. . . and **wild** *rice.*

Wild Rice

1½   cups water

1   tablespoon butter or margarine

⅛   teaspoon salt

1   2.75-ounce package quick-cooking wild rice

1   4-ounce can mushroom pieces

¼   cup chopped onion

2   tablespoons chopped celery

1   teaspoon dried parsley

1   small garlic clove, minced

In a saucepan, bring water, butter or margarine, and salt to a boil. Add rice, mushrooms, onion, celery, parsley, and garlic. Lower heat and simmer 10–15 minutes. Drain excess liquid. Fluff with a fork before serving. SERVES 4.

A salad of **artichoke hearts and sprouts** *was served on Lalique plates,*
as a separate course . . .

Hearts and Sprouts Salad

⅓   cup cider vinegar
⅓   cup sugar
¼   cup oil
⅛   teaspoon dried basil
¼   teaspoon salt
⅛   teaspoon pepper
2   6½-ounce jars marinated artichoke hearts, drained, not rinsed
1½   cups fresh sliced mushrooms
10   cherry tomatoes, halved
2   cups bean sprouts
4   ounces Farmer cheese, cubed
Boston lettuce

In a small saucepan, mix vinegar and sugar. Bring to a boil to dissolve the sugar. Let cool. Add oil, basil, salt, and pepper. In a bowl, lightly toss together artichoke hearts, mushrooms, tomatoes, bean sprouts, and cheese. Pour the vinegar/oil mixture over vegetable mixture. Chill. Serve on beds of Boston lettuce. SERVES 4.

. . . and the meal ended with a chocolate soufflé. Not bad, Qwilleran thought, for a crate-and-block environment.

Chocolate Soufflé

½ cup sugar
2 tablespoons cornstarch
¾ cup milk
2 ounces unsweetened chocolate
3 tablespoons butter or margarine
1 teaspoon vanilla extract
4 eggs, separated
sweetened whipped cream or whipped topping (optional)

Preheat oven to 350°. Place the sugar and cornstarch in a saucepan. Add the milk gradually while stirring. Cook over medium heat until the mixture thickens, stirring the entire time to prevent scorching. Take pan from the heat and add the chocolate, butter or margarine, and vanilla extract. Stir until chocolate is melted. Add the four egg yolks one at a time. Beat the mixture after each yolk is added. Let mixture cool. Beat the egg whites with an electric mixer until they reach the soft peak stage. Fold into chocolate mixture and pour into greased one-quart baking dish. Bake 45 minutes or until toothpick inserted in center comes out clean. Serve immediately with whipped cream or whipped topping, if desired. SERVES 4.

À La Carte

The . . . note was from Amberina: "Welcome to the Casablanca! Mary wants me to take you to dinner at Roberto's tonight."

. . . The antipasti were served . . .

"I wish my sisters could see me now!" said Amber. "Eating *squid* at Roberto's with a millionaire!"

Breaded Baby Squid

2–3 pounds baby squid
2 cups fine dry bread crumbs
¼ teaspoon salt
⅛ teaspoon pepper
1 teaspoon dried oregano or thyme
2 eggs, beaten
1 tablespoon milk
oil

Cut the arms from the heads of the squid. Discard the heads. Wash and drain. Combine the bread crumbs, salt, pepper, and spice. Mix the egg and milk. Dip the squid arms into the egg mixture, then into the bread crumb mixture. Fry in oil in a skillet until golden brown. Serve with hot marinara sauce. SERVES 4.

Marinara sauce:

- 1 clove garlic, minced
- 3 tablespoons oil
- 2¼ cups canned diced tomatoes
- 5 canned anchovies, chopped
- ¼ teaspoon oregano

Sauté the garlic in the oil. Add the tomatoes, anchovies, and oregano. Simmer for 10–15 minutes. Stir frequently. Add water if thinner sauce is desired.

The antipasto plates were whisked away, and the proficient waiter—who was always there when needed and absent when not—served the soup, a rich chicken broth threaded with egg and cheese.

Stracciatella Alla Romana

- 1 egg, beaten
- 2 teaspoons grated Parmesan cheese
- 1 tablespoon fine dry bread crumbs
- 1 small clove garlic, finely minced
- 2 14½-ounce cans chicken broth

Mix the egg, cheese, bread crumbs, and garlic together. Bring the chicken broth to a simmer. Quickly stir the egg mixture into the broth. Continue stirring until the egg is cooked. Serve immediately. SERVES 4.

"Here comes the veal."

Veal Rib Chop with Wine and Mushroom Sauce

4 veal chops
salt and pepper to taste
3 tablespoons oil
⅓ cup chopped onion
½ cup sliced mushrooms
2 tablespoons all-purpose flour
1 10½-ounce can beef broth
¼ cup water
½ cup red wine
2 tablespoons lemon juice

Preheat oven to 325°. Sprinkle chops with salt and pepper. Fry in oil until browned. Place chops in baking dish. Add onion and mushrooms to oil in skillet. Sauté. Stir in flour. Add beef broth, water, wine, and lemon juice. Cook until thickened, stirring constantly. Pour over chops. Cover and bake 1 hour or until chops are tender. SERVES 4.

Vitello Alla Piccata

---

4 thin veal scallops
⅓ cup all-purpose flour
¼ teaspoon garlic powder
salt and pepper to taste
¼ cup butter or margarine
½ lemon, juiced
1 tablespoon capers

Pound meat until flat. Mix the flour, garlic powder, salt, and pepper. Lightly dredge the meat in the flour mixture. Heat the butter or margarine in a skillet. Fry veal until golden brown. Remove from pan. Add lemon juice and capers to butter or margarine in skillet. Heat and pour over veal before serving. SERVES 4.

"Shall we have dessert? I recommend gelato and espresso."

Raspberry Cream Gelato

---

4 egg yolks
½ cup sugar
½ cup milk
1½ cups fresh or 12 ounces frozen raspberries
1 teaspoon powdered sugar
2 cups half-and-half
2 pounds rock salt
ice

Mix the egg yolks and sugar. Stir until the yolks turn a lighter color. Continue to stir while slowly adding the milk. Put the mixture into the top of a double boiler. Stir constantly. Cook until mixture coats the spoon. Do not allow mixture to boil. Remove from the heat at this point and continue to stir for 2 minutes. Transfer to a bowl to cool in the refrigerator for approximately 1 hour. Prepare the raspberries by pressing them through a sieve to remove seeds. Add the raspberry juice, powdered sugar, and half-and-half to the cold egg yolk mixture. Mix well. Place mixture in ice-cream maker. Follow the manufacturer's directions that accompany your machine. Place gelato into freezer section of refrigerator if it will not be served immediately. SERVES 4.

He sat on a stool at the counter, and the cashier insisted on serving him herself, while the cook waved a friendly hand in the small window of the kitchen door and later sent out a complimentary slice of **apple pie.**

Carriage House Café Apple Pie

Pastry:
- 2 cups all-purpose flour
- 1 teaspoon salt
- ⅔ cup shortening
- 5–6 tablespoons ice water

Mix flour and salt. Cut in shortening until mixture is about the size of small peas. Add water a tablespoonful at a time, mixing lightly with fork. When dough holds together, form into loose ball; divide in half. Roll 1 ball out to ¼ inch in thickness on floured surface.

Filling:

- 3 tablespoons butter or margarine, softened
- ⅓ cup pecan halves
- ⅓ cup shredded coconut
- 4–5 apples, peeled, sliced, parboiled
- ⅔ cup sugar
- 2 tablespoons all-purpose flour
- ¼ teaspoon nutmeg
- ½ teaspoon cinnamon
- ½ teaspoon salt

Preheat oven to 425°. Spread butter or margarine in a 9-inch pie pan. Place the pecans around the sides of the pie pan. Sprinkle bottom of pan with the coconut. Put dough into pan over the pecans and coconut. Combine the sugar, flour, nutmeg, cinnamon, and salt and stir into the drained apples. Place apples in pie pan. Roll out the remaining pastry and place it on top of the apples. Crimp edges to seal. Make slits in top crust to let steam escape. Bake 35 minutes or until golden brown. Let stand 3 minutes and then invert onto a serving plate. SERVES 6.

"Would you do me the honor of dining with me tonight at seven o'clock?
—Adelaide Plumb"

[This dinner was served by Ferdinand in the Casablanca, twelfth floor, for Countess Adelaide and Qwilleran] *on square-cut dinnerware on a round ebony table in a circular dining room paneled in black, turquoise, and mirror, its perimeter lighted with torchères. The entree was* shrimp Newburgh, *preceded by a slice of* pâté . . .

Pâté

———

1 stick of butter or margarine
1 large onion, finely chopped
1 pound of chicken livers
1 tablespoon Worcestershire sauce
1 teaspoon salt
¼ teaspoon pepper

Melt the butter or margarine in a skillet and add the onion. Cook until transparent. Add the livers and cook about 6 minutes or until livers are cooked through. Put butter or margarine, onion, and livers into a food processor and process until smooth. Add the Worcestershire sauce, salt, and pepper. Process 20 seconds longer. Press the mixture into a small loaf pan greased with butter or margarine. Chill and turn out onto a plate for slicing. MAKES 10–12 SERVINGS.

Shrimp Newburgh

2 tablespoons butter or margarine
2 tablespoons all-purpose flour
½ teaspoon salt
dash of red pepper
1 cup light cream
2 egg yolks, beaten
1¾ cups cooked shrimp
2 tablespoons sherry
4 rounds of puff pastry

Melt the butter or margarine in a saucepan. Add the flour, salt, and red pepper. Stir and then add cream. Cook, stirring constantly, until the mixture is thick. Very slowly stir part of the hot cream mixture into the egg yolks. Return egg yolks and cream mixture to the saucepan. Reduce heat. Add shrimp and sherry; heat through but do not boil. Serve over the rounds of puff pastry. SERVES 4.

NOTE: There are excellent frozen rounds of puff pastry available in the frozen food section of most grocery stores.

Then Ferdinand prepared **bananas Foster** *in a chafing dish with heavy-handed competence and a disdainful expression meaning that this was not real food.*

Bananas Foster

4   ripened large bananas, peeled
1   stick butter or margarine
¾   cup brown sugar, packed
¼   cup rum
vanilla ice cream

Cut bananas lengthwise and again crosswise. Melt the butter or margarine in a skillet or chafing dish. Add the brown sugar; stir, and add the banana quarters. Stir and cook 2 to 3 minutes. Heat the rum in a small pan. Pour over the bananas and ignite. Serve immediately over vanilla ice cream. SERVES 4.

"The maid was kind of weird, but the housekeeper's nice," Amber informed him [Qwilleran] . . .

"She commutes daily to Twelve, where she bakes her famous caraway seed cake," Courtney added.

Famous Caraway Seed Cake

½ cup butter, softened
¾ cup sugar
1 teaspoon vanilla extract
3 eggs
2 cups all-purpose flour
2 teaspoons baking powder
½ teaspoon salt
¼ teaspoon nutmeg
2 teaspoons caraway seeds
½ cup half-and-half
sugar

Preheat oven to 350°. Cream the butter and sugar until light and fluffy. Add the vanilla extract and the eggs, one at a time. Beat well after addition of each egg. Sift or mix the flour, baking powder, salt, and nutmeg in another bowl. Add the caraway seeds to the dry ingredients. Add the dry ingredients to the butter and sugar mixture, alternating with the half-and-half. Pour into a greased and sugared 5-inch by 9-inch loaf pan. Bake for 45–50 minutes. Cool for 10 minutes in the pan. Turn out on rack to finish cooling. SERVES 6–8.

*"Would you like a **margarita**, angel?" the host* [Courtney] *asked.*

"It would pleasure me immensely." [answered Winifred] *She sat on the army cot next to Qwilleran, who was aware of a heady scent and long silky legs.*

Margarita

slice of lemon
salt
1½ ounces tequila
½ ounce triple sec
½ lemon, juiced
ice cubes

Moisten the rim of a cocktail glass with the lemon slice. Sprinkle salt over the rim. Shake the tequila, triple sec, lemon juice, and ice cubes vigorously in cocktail shaker. Strain into glass.

Qwilleran went to the deli for an early dinner. All he wanted was a bowl of chicken soup with matzo balls, a pastrami sandwich two inches thick, a dish of rice pudding, and some time to sort out his feelings about life in the big city.

Big-City Rice Pudding

2   cups + 2 cups milk
¾   cup uncooked rice
½   cup raisins
¼   cup butter or margarine
3   eggs, beaten
½   cup sugar
1   teaspoon vanilla
½   teaspoon salt
⅛   teaspoon ground cinnamon
ground nutmeg

Preheat oven to 325°. In a saucepan bring 2 cups milk, rice, and raisins to a boil. Reduce heat. Cover and cook over very low heat for 15 minutes. Remove from heat and stir in butter or margarine until melted. In a bowl, combine eggs, remaining 2 cups milk, sugar, vanilla, salt, and cinnamon. Slowly stir rice mixture into egg mixture. Place in greased 10-inch by 6-inch by 2-inch baking dish. Sprinkle with nutmeg. Bake 45–50 minutes or until knife inserted in center comes out clean. Serve with cream or milk, if desired. SERVES 6.

The Cat Who Knew a Cardinal

More than apple trees grow in Qwilleran's orchard. There's a mystery growing when the director of the Pickax Theatre Club's Shakespeare production is found dead among the trees! With the help of Koko, Qwill identifies the murderer.

Dinner at the Old Stone Mill

Dinner Rolls

Chicken Gumbo

Halibut Steaks

Broccoli Spears with Bacon Horseradish Sauce

Old Stone Mill Squash Soufflé

🐾

It was a short drive to the Old Stone Mill on the outskirts of town, and they [Qwilleran and Polly] filled the time with comments on the weather: the highs and lows, humidity and visibility, yesterday and today. At the restaurant they were shown to Qwilleran's favorite table, and he ordered the usual dry sherry for Polly and the usual Squunk water for himself.

*"We'll have the **soup** served right away." He signaled the waitress. "Eat a **roll**. I'll butter it for you."*

Dinner Rolls

½ cup sugar
½ cup shortening
1 teaspoon salt
2 eggs
2 packages dry yeast
¾ cup lukewarm milk (105–115°)
3½ cups all-purpose flour
butter

With a mixer, combine sugar, shortening, salt, and eggs. Add yeast to milk. Stir to dissolve. Mix yeast mixture into egg mixture. Still using the mixer, add 2 cups of the flour slowly, one at a time, being sure to scrape the sides of the bowl. Stir in the last 1½ cups of flour by hand. Again, scrape the sides of the bowl. Knead 3 or 4 times on a lightly floured surface to make a smooth dough. Place in a lightly greased bowl. Turn once to coat the top of the dough with shortening. Cover with a cloth and let rise until doubled in bulk, approximately 1 hour. Punch down and roll out into 2 circles ¼ inch in thickness and approximately 12 inches in diameter. Spread with butter. Cut into 12 triangles by cutting each circle into fourths and each fourth into three equal triangles.

Roll up each triangle beginning with the long side, butterhorn style. Place seam side down on an ungreased baking sheet. Cover and let rise again until doubled in bulk, approximately 45 minutes. Brush tops of rolls with butter and bake at 400° for 10 to 12 minutes. MAKES 24.

When the chicken gumbo *was served and she had revived, he went on.*
"Do you realize this is our first dinner together in ten days?"

Chicken Gumbo

2 tablespoons butter or margarine
2 tablespoons olive oil
1 onion, chopped
1 large clove garlic, chopped
1 14½-ounce can diced tomatoes
½ cup chopped green pepper
1 cup canned, frozen, or fresh okra
3 tablespoons rice, uncooked
3 14½-ounce cans chicken broth
   salt and pepper to taste
½ teaspoon dried tarragon
1 bay leaf
2 cups chicken, cooked, diced

Heat butter or margarine and olive oil in large saucepan. Sauté onion and garlic. Add tomatoes, green pepper, okra, rice, broth, salt, pepper, tarragon, and bay leaf. Stir. Simmer, covered, about 25 minutes or until vegetables are tender. Add chicken. Simmer for 10 minutes. Remove bay leaf before serving. SERVES 4–6.

The halibut steaks arrived . . .

Halibut Steaks

¼ cup chopped green pepper
1   clove garlic, chopped
3   tablespoons butter or oil
3   tablespoons onion soup mix
½   cup water
½   cup ketchup
½   teaspoon sugar
2   8-ounce halibut steaks
salt and pepper to taste

Preheat oven to 375°. Sauté green pepper and garlic in butter or oil. Add soup mix, water, ketchup, and sugar. Simmer 5 minutes. Place halibut steaks in baking dish. Add salt and pepper. Cover with sauce and bake, covered, for 20 minutes. SERVES 2.

Broccoli Spears with Bacon Horseradish Sauce

3 tablespoons butter or margarine, melted
¾ cup mayonnaise
1 tablespoon prepared horseradish
1 tablespoon finely chopped onion
¼ teaspoon garlic salt
1 head of fresh broccoli spears
2 slices bacon, cooked and crumbled

Combine butter or margarine, mayonnaise, horseradish, onion, and garlic salt. Refrigerate several hours. Cut broccoli into spears, and steam until heated through but still crisp. Drain and place on serving plate. Warm sauce; stir bacon into sauce just before serving. SERVES 4.

Old Stone Mill Squash Soufflé

2 pounds yellow crookneck squash, chopped
water
5 tablespoons butter or margarine, melted
⅔ cup milk
2 eggs, beaten
2 teaspoons all-purpose flour
3 tablespoons sugar
1 tablespoon baking powder
¾ cup finely chopped onion

1   teaspoon salt

¼   teaspoon pepper

Preheat oven to 400°. Cook squash in small amount of water until tender. Drain. Mash lightly in bowl. Add butter or margarine. Mix milk, eggs, flour, sugar, baking powder, onion, salt, and pepper with mixer. Add squash. Stir well and pour into 8½-inch by 11-inch greased baking pan. Bake for 30 minutes or until squash is set. SERVES 6–8.

À La Carte

"Would you like a drink of Scotch and a bowl of chili *first?"* [asked Qwilleran] . . .

After the bowls of chili (hot) and coffee (strong), Qwilleran helped carry the photographic equipment to the van.

Chili

1   pound stew beef or any lean beef chunks

water for boiling meat

2   medium onions, chopped

2   garlic cloves, chopped

1   10¾-ounce can puréed tomatoes

1   15½-ounce can tomato sauce

2   15½-ounce cans kidney beans

chili powder to taste

Place meat in large saucepan. Cover with water and boil until almost tender. Drain, reserving 1 cup of broth. Add onions, garlic, tomatoes, tomato sauce, reserved broth, kidney beans, and chili powder. Mix well. Simmer approximately 1 hour, adding more water, if necessary, to adjust to desired consistency. SERVES 6.

Compton . . . said, "What looks interesting on the menu? I don't want anything nutritious. I get all that at home." The superintendent was a painfully thin man who smoked too many cigars and scoffed at vegetables and salads.

Qwilleran said, "There's a **cheese and broccoli soup** *that's so thick you could use it for mortar. The avocado-stuffed pita is a mess to eat, but delicious. The* **crab Louis salad** *is the genuine thing."*

Cheese and Broccoli Soup

———————

3 tablespoons chopped onion
5 tablespoons butter or margarine
5 tablespoons all-purpose flour
2 14½-ounce cans chicken broth
1 10-ounce package frozen chopped broccoli
2 medium potatoes, diced
salt and pepper to taste
1 cup American or cheddar cheese, grated
2 cups half-and-half
milk (optional)
flour (optional)

Sauté the onion in the butter or margarine in a large saucepan. Stir in the flour. Gradually pour in the broth, stirring over medium heat until thick. Add broccoli, potatoes, salt, and pepper. Simmer until vegetables are tender. Add cheese and half-and-half. Simmer until cheese melts. Do not boil. Additional flour mixed with a little milk can be added at this point to thicken to the "mortar" state, if desired. SERVES 4.

Crab Louis Salad

2   6-ounce cans crabmeat, or ¾ pound fresh crabmeat, cooked, flaked
½   cup finely chopped celery
¼   cup thinly sliced pimento-stuffed olives
lettuce
Louis dressing
4   hard-boiled eggs, quartered
4   tomatoes, quartered
ripe olives
whole crab legs (optional)

Combine the crabmeat, celery, and pimento-stuffed olives. Arrange on lettuce. Top with Louis dressing. Garnish with eggs, tomatoes, ripe olives, and crab legs, if desired. SERVES 4.

Louis dressing:
½   cup chili sauce
½   cup mayonnaise
¼   cup heavy cream
¼   teaspoon Worcestershire sauce
2   teaspoons lemon juice
salt and pepper to taste

Place chili sauce, mayonnaise, and cream in a small bowl and mix well. Add Worcestershire sauce, lemon juice, salt, and pepper, stir. Refrigerate until serving time.

Bushy backed into the parking slot designated G-12, with the tail of the van down-slope. Chairs and snack tables were set up on the downside, and he [Bushy] went about mixing drinks. "Bloody Mary okay for everybody?" he asked.

"You know how I want mine," Qwilleran said.

"Right. Extra hot, two stalks of celery, and no vodka."

Bloody Mary

---

dash Worcestershire sauce
2 drops Tabasco sauce
½ ounce lemon juice
salt and pepper to taste
1½ ounces vodka
tomato juice
celery stalk

In a 10-ounce glass mix Worcestershire sauce, Tabasco sauce, and lemon juice. Stir in salt and pepper. Stir in vodka; add ice cubes. Pour in tomato juice and stir with celery stalk.

He introduced his guests, all connected with the newspaper, and the women busied themselves with the food. Joining with the Bushlands they set up a tailgate spread of ham, potato salad, baked beans, coleslaw, olives, dill pickles, pumpkin tarts, and chocolate cake.

Potato Salad

---

1 cup mayonnaise
⅛ cup mustard
¼ cup finely chopped onion
½ cup finely chopped celery
5 medium-sized potatoes, cooked and diced
salt and pepper to taste
3 hard-boiled eggs, diced
½ cup sweet pickle relish

Combine mayonnaise, mustard, onion, and celery. Gently stir mixture into potatoes. Add salt and pepper. Then fold in eggs and relish. SERVES 6.

Tailgate Coleslaw

2 cups shredded red cabbage
2 cups shredded green cabbage
¼ cup finely chopped onion
⅔ cup mayonnaise
2 tablespoons sugar
2 tablespoons cider vinegar
pepper to taste
½ teaspoon celery salt

Combine cabbages and onion. In a separate bowl, stir together mayonnaise, sugar, vinegar, pepper, and celery salt. Pour over cabbage mixture. Mix well. SERVES 4–6.

Easy Chocolate Cake

1½ cups all-purpose flour
1 cup sugar
2 teaspoons + 2 tablespoons cocoa
1 teaspoon baking soda
½ teaspoon salt
6 tablespoons oil
1 teaspoon vanilla extract
1 tablespoon vinegar
1 cup cold water
1 cup whipping cream
2 tablespoons sugar
½ teaspoon vanilla extract

Preheat oven to 350°. Grease an 8-inch square cake pan; dust with the 2 teaspoons of cocoa. Sift or mix flour, sugar, the 2 tablespoons cocoa, baking soda, and salt together. Place in medium-sized mixing bowl. Make 3 holes in the flour mixture. Put oil in the first hole, vanilla extract in the second hole, and vinegar in the third hole. Pour the water over all of it. Stir with fork until blended. Pour into prepared pan. Bake about 35 minutes. Let cool in pan 5 minutes. Invert and remove. Whip cream. Add sugar and vanilla. (Whipped topping can be substituted for whipped cream.) Spread on cake when cool. SERVES 6–8.

On Saturday he [Qwilleran] wanted Polly to fly to Chicago for a ball game; she wanted to go birding in the wetlands. They compromised on a picnic lunch—with binoculars—on the banks of the Ittibittiwassee River.

*. . . He loaded a limp paper plate with moist **tuna sandwiches** and hard-cooked eggs with moist stuffing, neither of which was compatible with an oversized moustache.*

Polly's Tuna Sandwiches

1   6-ounce can tuna, drained
⅛   cup finely chopped onion
2   hard-boiled eggs, finely chopped
1   teaspoon lemon juice
2   tablespoons mayonnaise
3   tablespoons sweet pickle relish
4   slices sourdough bread
    lettuce
    tomato

Mix tuna, onion, eggs, lemon juice, mayonnaise, and relish. Spread on 2 slices of the bread. Top with lettuce, tomato, and remaining 2 slices of the bread. MAKES 2 SANDWICHES.

"And I made chocolate brownies." [said Polly]

After several **brownies** *Qwilleran was feeling more agreeable. In a mellow mood he murmured, "This is supposed to be our last warm weekend."*

"I've enjoyed our picnic," she said. "I've enjoyed every minute of it."

"So have I. We belong together, Polly."

"I'm happiest when I'm with you, Qwill."

Polly's Picnic Brownies

---

4   1-ounce squares baking chocolate
¾   cup butter or margarine
6   eggs, beaten
3   cups sugar
2   cups all-purpose flour
1   teaspoon salt
2   teaspoons vanilla extract
1   cup chopped nuts

Preheat oven to 350°. Melt chocolate with butter or margarine. Cool slightly. In a large bowl, beat eggs and sugar together. Combine flour and salt with egg mixture. Stir chocolate mixture into flour and egg mixture. Add vanilla extract and nuts. Pour into greased and floured 11-inch by 15-inch pan. Bake 30–35 minutes. Spread with frosting. Cut into squares. SERVES 8–10.

Frosting:

- ⅓ cup butter, softened
- ½ cup cocoa
- 4 cups powdered sugar
- ⅓ cup milk
- 1 teaspoon vanilla extract

Beat butter until fluffy. Add cocoa and beat until well-blended. Add powdered sugar alternately with milk. Beat until smooth. Blend in vanilla extract.

The Cat Who Moved a Mountain

Qwilleran is now a billionaire! He owns property from New Jersey to Nevada but decides to rent a house for himself and the cats in the Potato Mountains. When he gets there he finds himself in the middle of a fight between the mountain residents and the developers.

Lunch Bucket Lunch

Vegetable Soup

❖

Veggieburgers

❖

Amy's Oat Bran Cookies

At the Lunch Bucket the plump and pretty proprietor was behind the high counter, smiling as usual, and the baby was burbling in his basket . . .

*Qwilleran ordered soup and a **veggieburger** . . .*

*She ladled up a bowl of **vegetable soup** . . . It was thick with vegetables, including turnips, which he swallowed without complaint. "Excellent soup, Amy! A person could live on this stuff."*

Vegetable Soup

2	14½-ounce cans vegetable broth
½	cup chopped onion
½	cup chopped celery
1	clove garlic, minced
1	cup sliced carrots
½	cup diced turnips
1	cup diced potatoes
1	bay leaf (optional)
¼	cup barley
	salt and pepper to taste

Place all ingredients in a saucepan and simmer, covered, until vegetables are tender and barley is cooked. Remove bay leaf before serving. SERVES 4–6.

Veggieburger

1¼   cups shredded cheddar cheese
1   medium onion, chopped
1   small clove garlic, minced
1   cup bread crumbs
1   cup finely chopped pecans
1   egg, beaten
2   tablespoons chili sauce
1   teaspoon dried basil
salt and pepper to taste
canola oil
6   hamburger rolls

Place all ingredients except oil and buns in a bowl and mix well. Shape into 6 patties. If mixture doesn't hold together, add a little milk. Fry in oil until lightly browned on both sides. Serve on rolls with condiment(s) of choice. SERVES 6.

Qwilleran accepted coffee substitute and two oat bran cookies.

Amy's Oat Bran Cookies

½   cup brown sugar, packed
½   cup butter or margarine, softened
2   eggs
¼   cup molasses
½   teaspoon baking soda
½   teaspoon baking powder

1   teaspoon ginger

1   teaspoon cinnamon

½   teaspoon ground cloves

¼   teaspoon salt

1   cup oat bran

2   cups all-purpose flour

Preheat oven to 350°. Cream sugar and butter or margarine. Add eggs, beating well after each egg. Add molasses, baking soda, baking powder, spices, and salt. Mix well. Stir in oat bran and flour. Drop by rounded teaspoonsful onto greased cookie sheet. Bake 8–10 minutes. MAKES ABOUT 40 COOKIES.

À La Carte

At the Five Points Café the Father's Day Special was a turkey dinner with **cornbread dressing**, *cranberry sauce, and* **nips**.

Cornbread Dressing

3	cups cornbread crumbs
20	slices fresh or day-old bread, torn into small pieces
1	cup chopped onion
1	cup chopped celery
5	eggs, beaten
½	cup milk
1	teaspoon salt
1	teaspoon pepper
2	tablespoons poultry seasoning
	hot water

Preheat oven to 375°. Mix all ingredients except water. While stirring, add enough hot water to the bread mixture to make a thick, souplike consistency. Pour mixture into a greased 8½-inch by 11-inch pan. Bake about 45 minutes. Cut into squares to serve. SERVES 4–6.

🐾

(Tur)Nips

3 cups peeled, diced turnips
milk, warm
2 tablespoons butter or margarine, melted
salt and pepper to taste

Boil turnips until tender. Drain. Using electric mixer, beat turnips, adding milk to desired consistency, butter or margarine, salt, and pepper. SERVES 4.

"Come into the family room, Jim, and meet your neighbors from Tiptop Estates. May I call you Jim? Please call me Dolly."

"My friends call me Qwill," he said.

"Oh, I like that! What will you have to drink?"

"What are you having?"

"My downfall—brandy and soda."

"I'll have the same—on ice—without the brandy."

Brandy and Soda

ice cubes
2½ ounces brandy
6 ounces club soda

Place several ice cubes in a 12-ounce glass. Pour brandy and soda over ice. Stir gently.

Separating the bakery from the snack area was a scarred glass case displaying cookies, muffins, Danish pastries, and pecan rolls, although very little of each . . .

Qwilleran helped himself to coffee and bought an **apple Danish** from the baker. Qwilleran carried his purchase to an orchid student chair and bit into a six-inch square of puffy, chewy pastry heaped with large apple slices in thick and spicy juices. It was still warm.

"I'm forced to tell you," he said, "that this is absolutely the best Danish I've ever eaten in half a century of pastry connoisseurship."

Apple Danish

————————

2 apples, peeled, cored, sliced
1 cup water
1 cup sugar
⅛ teaspoon cinnamon
dash nutmeg
2 tablespoons cornstarch
2 tablespoons cold water
6 puff pastry shells, thawed to room temperature
all-purpose flour

Glaze:
1 cup powdered sugar
milk
¼ teaspoon vanilla or almond extract

Preheat oven to 400°. Place apples, water, sugar, cinnamon, and nutmeg in a saucepan over medium heat. Simmer uncovered until apples are tender. Mix cornstarch with water, add to apple mixture. Stir gently until thick and bubbly, being careful not to break up apple slices. Remove from heat. Place thawed pastry shells on a floured surface. Roll out each into a 6-inch square. Place on two ungreased cookie sheets. Divide filling among pastry shells. Spoon filling into center of each shell leaving a ½-inch margin around outside of shell. Bake for 25 minutes or until lightly browned and puffy. Cool slightly. Mix powdered sugar with enough milk to make a thin glaze. Add vanilla or almond extract. Drizzle over pastries. SERVES 6.

[Having been in an accident] *Qwilleran slid downstairs to feed the Siamese and make a breakfast of* **sticky buns**.

Sticky Buns

1   package dry yeast
¼   cup warm water (105–115°)
1   cup milk, scalded
¼   cup shortening + additional shortening for brushing on top of dough
¼   cup sugar
1   teaspoon salt
4   cups all-purpose flour
1   beaten egg

Topping:
1   cup brown sugar, packed
½   cup butter or margarine
2   tablespoons light corn syrup
⅔   cup pecans

Filling:

- ¼ cup butter or margarine, softened
- ½ cup sugar
- 1 teaspoon cinnamon

Soften dry yeast in warm water. Combine hot milk, shortening, sugar, and salt. Cool to luke-warm. Add 1 cup of the flour. Beat well. Add softened yeast and egg. Add remaining flour gradually to form a soft dough. Shape into a ball and place into a greased bowl. Brush the top lightly with additional melted shortening. Cover and let rise in a warm place until doubled. In a saucepan, mix together ingredients for topping. Heat slowly, stirring until blended. Pour into greased 9-inch by 13-inch pan. When dough is doubled, approximately 1 hour, punch down and turn out onto a lightly floured surface. Dough will be sticky. Divide dough in half. Roll each piece into a 10-inch by 12-inch rectangle. Brush each rectangle with the softened butter or margarine. Use more butter or margarine, if necessary, to cover both rectangles. Combine sugar and cinnamon. Sprinkle half over each rectangle. Beginning with the long side, roll each in jelly-roll fashion. Seal edge with a little water. Cut each roll into eight 1½-inch slices. Place slices in pan on topping, cut side down. Cover and let rise till doubled, approximately 45 minutes. Bake at 350° for about 25 minutes or until lightly browned. Cool 2 minutes and invert on serving dish. SERVES 8.

"Come in," he [Qwilleran] *said, exaggerating his limp and his facial expressions of agony.*

"Colin told me about your misfortune, and I brought you some of my Chocolate Whoppers *to boost your morale." She [Vonda Dudley Wix] was holding a paper plate covered with foil.*

Qwilleran . . . unwrapped the cookies: three inches in diameter, an inch thick, and loaded with morsels of chocolate and chunks of walnuts.

"They're a trifle excessive," said his guest, "but that's how my boss liked them."

Vonda's Chocolate Whoppers

2¼ cups all-purpose flour
1 teaspoon baking powder
½ teaspoon salt
¾ cup sugar
¾ cup brown sugar, packed
½ cup shortening
½ cup butter or margarine
1½ teaspoons vanilla extract
2 eggs
4 squares unsweetened baking chocolate, melted and cooled
1 10-ounce package semi-sweet chocolate chunks
1½ cups walnuts

Preheat oven to 375°. Sift or mix flour, baking powder, and salt together and put aside. Beat sugars, shortening, and butter or margarine until light and fluffy with electric mixer. Add vanilla extract and eggs, beating after each egg. Add unsweetened baking chocolate and the dry ingredients to the sugar mixture and mix well. Fold in chocolate chunks and walnuts, mixing by hand. Drop by ¼ cupfuls onto ungreased cookie sheets. Bake 12–14 minutes. MAKES 18 WHOPPERS.

He waved his guests into the living room. "What may I serve you to drink?" [asked Qwilleran]

"Qwill makes a super Manhattan," Sherry said as she settled familiarly on the sofa.

Manhattan

1½ ounces Canadian whisky
¾   ounce Italian vermouth
2   dashes Angostura bitters
    ice cubes

Stir whisky, vermouth, and bitters with the ice cubes. Strain into a cocktail glass.

The Cat Who Wasn't There

Qwilleran becomes a jet-setter and heads for Scotland. Is he researching his roots or is he just a tourist? Little does he know, one of his traveling companions won't be coming back. Koko seems to know all about it even though he wasn't there.

Anglo-Indian Supper

Samosas

Mulligatawny Soup

Tandoori Murghi

Pulao

Tarka Dal

The restaurant, in true Anglo-Indian style, had white tile floors, tinkling fountains, hanging brass lamps, an assertive aroma of curry, and a background of raga music played on the sarod, tabla, and tamboura. The plucked strings, rhythmic percussion, and hypnotic drone of the instruments provided a soothing background for conversation . . . Qwilleran suggested ordering *samosas* with the drinks, saying they were meat-filled pastries. Then he recommended *mulligatawny soup* and a main course of *tandoori murghi* and *pulao*, with a side order of *dal.* "All spicy dishes, I don't need to tell you," he warned.

"Why, this is nothing but roast chicken with rice and lentils," Amanda announced when the entree was served.

Samosas

¼ teaspoon mustard seeds
oil
1 dried red chili, chopped
1 4-ounce can chopped green chili
1 medium onion, chopped
½ teaspoon turmeric
1 teaspoon coriander
½ teaspoon cumin
½ pound lamb, ground, cooked
2 medium potatoes, peeled, boiled, finely diced
salt to taste

Pastry:

- 4 tablespoons butter
- 2 cups all-purpose flour
- ½ teaspoon salt
- 5 tablespoons warm water

Heat the mustard seeds in 2 tablespoons oil until they crack open. Add the red chili, green chili, and onion. Cook until onions are soft. Add the turmeric, coriander, cumin, lamb, potatoes, and salt. Stir over medium heat 3–5 minutes. Set aside. To make pastry, cut butter into flour and salt. Add the water. Mix with fork until dough clings together. Divide into 9 balls and then flatten each ball into a circle about 4 inches in diameter. Cut in half and form into a "cone" by folding in half. Put about a teaspoon of the filling into each cone. Put a little water on any edges that have difficulty joining and press together firmly. Fry in oil until golden brown. MAKES 18.

Mulligatawny Soup

- 1 medium onion, chopped
- 1 carrot, chopped
- 1 stalk celery, chopped
- 1 tart apple, peeled, cored, chopped
- oil
- 1½ tablespoons all-purpose flour
- 2–3 teaspoons curry powder
- ⅛ teaspoon dried thyme
- 2 14½-ounce cans chicken broth
- salt and pepper to taste
- 2 tablespoons shredded coconut
- 5 tablespoons rice, uncooked
- ½ cup chicken, cooked, chopped

Sauté the onion, carrot, celery, and apple in oil. Stir in the flour, curry powder, and thyme. Add chicken broth, stirring until well-blended. Add salt, pepper, coconut, rice, and chicken. Simmer, covered, for 30 minutes. SERVES 4.

Tandoori Murghi (Chicken)

1 teaspoon ginger
1 teaspoon allspice
½ teaspoon crushed red pepper
1 tablespoon lemon juice
2 cloves garlic, minced
3 teaspoons all-purpose flour
4 chicken breasts, with skin
yogurt, plain

Make a paste of the spices, lemon juice, garlic, and flour. Lift the skins of the chicken breasts and spread about a teaspoon of the paste between the skin and the meat. Chicken can be grilled, broiled, or baked. If grilling or broiling, place about 6 inches from the source of heat. Turn often. Cook until tender—about 30 minutes. If baking, place in baking dish and cover. Bake at 350° until tender—about 45 minutes. Spoon cold yogurt over chicken when served. Serve with pulao. SERVES 4.

Pulao (Rice)

⅓ cup butter or margarine
1   cup rice, uncooked
¾ cup chopped onion
½ teaspoon salt
1   teaspoon curry powder
⅓ cup raisins
¼ cup sliced almonds
½ cup water
1   14½-ounce can chicken broth

Preheat oven to 350°. Melt butter or margarine in skillet. Add uncooked rice and onion. Cook, stirring occasionally until onion is tender. Add salt, curry powder, raisins, and almonds. Place in 1½-quart buttered baking dish. Combine water and broth and bring to a boil. Pour over rice mixture. Stir and cover. Bake until liquid is absorbed—about 35 minutes. SERVES 4.

Tarka Dal (Spiced Lentils)

¾ cup red lentils (available at most health food stores)
1   teaspoon turmeric
½ teaspoon cumin
½ teaspoon salt
3½ cups water
1   onion, chopped fine
1   large clove garlic, minced
dried red chilies to taste, chopped
2   tablespoons butter or margarine

Place lentils, turmeric, cumin, and salt in water and bring to a boil over medium-high heat. Then lower the heat and simmer, uncovered, about 10 minutes, stirring often. Cover the pan and simmer an additional 30 minutes, stirring occasionally. Cool slightly and puree in a food processer. Sauté the onion, garlic, and chilies in butter or margarine. Add to the lentils. Do not process after adding onion mixture. SERVES 4.

À La Carte

*They dressed, packed, put their luggage out in the hall, and reported for breakfast at seven o'clock. No one was really hungry, and they were dismayed by the array of oatmeal, **eggs**, meat, fish, fruit, pancakes, scones, currant buns, oatcakes, bannocks, jams, marmalade, and more.*

Scotch Eggs

4 hard-boiled eggs, shells removed
1 egg, beaten
1 pound ground sausage
¾ cup fine dry bread crumbs
oil

Dip the hard-boiled eggs into beaten egg. Shape a generous coating of sausage around each egg. Dip into beaten egg again; roll in the bread crumbs. Deep fry at 375° 5–6 minutes or fry in a skillet, turning frequently. SERVES 4.

After breakfasting on a compote of dried apple slices, prunes, and figs, followed by creamed finnan haddie and oatcakes, the group shook hands with the innkeeper and his wife and prepared to board the bus in the courtyard of the inn.

Fruit Compote

————

1½   cups dried apples
½   cup pitted prunes
½   cup dried figs
3½   cups water
3   tablespoons sugar
3   teaspoons lemon juice

Cut the dried fruits into small pieces. Place in the water and bring to a boil. Lower the heat, cover, and simmer about 15 minutes. Add sugar and lemon juice, continuing to simmer just until sugar is dissolved. Can be served warm or cold. SERVES 4.

Creamed Finnan Haddie

————

1   large onion, thinly sliced
1   pound smoked haddock
1¾   cups milk
¼   teaspoon pepper
1½   teaspoons dry mustard
4   tablespoons butter, room temperature
2   teaspoons all-purpose flour

Spread onion over the bottom of a large saucepan. Cut haddock into 1-inch wide pieces. Place on top of onion. Mix milk, pepper, and mustard. Pour over the haddock and slowly bring to a boil. Reduce heat to low; simmer, covered, for 5 minutes. Remove cover and simmer 6 minutes. Remove fish and place in warm oven on serving plate. Combine butter and flour. Add to pan in which fish was cooked. Stir constantly until slightly thickened. Pour over fish and serve. SERVES 4.

Oatcakes

1   cup quick-cooking oats
½   cup shortening
1   cup all-purpose flour
½   teaspoon salt
½   teaspoon baking soda
2–3   tablespoons ice water
jelly or cheese (optional)

Preheat oven to 350°. Mix the oats, shortening, flour, salt, and baking soda thoroughly. Add the water, a little at a time, until a stiff dough is formed. Roll out to about ⅛ inch in thickness on a floured surface. Cut into rounds using a cookie cutter or drinking glass. Bake on ungreased cookie sheet 12–15 minutes. Can be served with jelly or cheese. MAKES ABOUT 18 CAKES.

The waiter marched into the room and set the tray on a lace-covered tea table in front of a stiff little settee. The tray was laden with porcelain cups and saucers, a rosebud-patterned china teapot, a silver milk and sugar service, a plate of shortbread, and dainty embroidered napkins in silver rings.

Shortbread

1	cup butter, softened
⅔	cup powdered sugar
½	teaspoon vanilla extract
2	cups all-purpose flour

Preheat oven to 325°. Beat butter until light. Add powdered sugar and vanilla extract. Using a rubber scraper to stir, add the flour. Roll into small balls and flatten. Prick with fork. Or press into 8-inch square baking dish to a depth of ½ inch. Prick with fork. Bake 20–30 minutes or until golden brown. SERVES 4.

To fortify himself for the appointment he had a good lunch at the Old Stone Mill—crab bisque, a Reuben sandwich, pumpkin pie—and before driving to Goodwinter Boulevard he picked up a bunch of mums at the florist shop.

Crab Bisque

¼ cup finely diced celery
⅛ cup finely diced onion
3 tablespoons butter or margarine
3 tablespoons flour
4 cups milk
2 cups cream
1 pound white crabmeat
salt and pepper to taste
sherry to taste

Sauté the celery and onion until tender in the butter or margarine. Stir flour into the onions and celery. Slowly add the milk, stirring constantly over medium heat until thickened. Stir in cream and crabmeat. Add salt, pepper, and sherry. Do not boil. SERVES 6–8.

The Italian trattoria in Mooseville was one of the county's few ethnic restaurants—a small mama-and-papa establishment in a storefront with a homemade sign. Mrs. Linguini gave them the best of the eleven tables and then stood staring at the four of them with one fist on her hip. That was Linguini body language for "What do you want from the bar?"

There were no menu cards and everyone in the restaurant had to eat what Mr. Linguini felt like cooking on that particular evening.

"*Bagna cauda!*" she announced. "You dip it. *Verra nice . . .* Zuppa di fagioli! . . . *Verra nice . . .* Tortellini quattro formaggi . . . *Verra nice . . . Polpettone alla bolognese! Verra nice . . .* Zuccotto! *Verra nice.*"

Bagna Cauda (Garlic and Anchovy Dip)

4   ounces canned salted anchovies or 4 ounces anchovy paste
4   tablespoons unsalted butter
4   cloves garlic, chopped
1¼   cups olive oil
raw vegetables

Chop and mash the anchovies into a smooth consistency. Melt the butter in a fondue pot over low heat on the stove or in a skillet. Add the garlic. Cook a few minutes and then add the anchovies. Add the olive oil and simmer about 10 minutes. If using a fondue pot, place it on the flame at this point. If not using a pot, pour the mixture into a serving dish. Dip raw vegetables such as cauliflower, broccoli, green, red, and yellow peppers into it. SERVES 4.

Polpettone Alla Bolognese (Meat loaf)

1   onion, chopped
2   tablespoons butter or margarine
1   pound ground beef
2   tablespoons Parmesan cheese
⅛   teaspoon cinnamon
½   teaspoon salt
¼   teaspoon pepper
¼   cup fine fresh bread crumbs
1   egg, beaten
1   lemon, juiced
6   tablespoons milk (approximately)
5   tablespoons oil

Preheat oven to 375°. Sauté onions in butter or margarine and place on bottom of baking dish or loaf pan. Mix the beef, cheese, cinnamon, salt, pepper, half the bread crumbs, egg, lemon juice, and enough milk to make a moist mixture that is not sticky. Form the meat into a loaf and roll it in the rest of the bread crumbs. Heat oil in a pan. Brown loaf over high heat. Place the loaf on onions and bake 35–40 minutes. Invert to serve. SERVES 4–6.

The Cat Who Went into the Closet

Qwilleran has moved into an old mansion that boasts fifty closets filled with junk. The owners never threw anything away—not even champagne corks. Now the cats and Qwill must explore the contents of all those closets as he investigates the deaths of two people. Could there be a murderer lurking nearby?

Thanksgiving Dinner

Roast Turkey

Autumn Stuffing

Squash Puree

Thanksgiving Potatoes

Mildred's Mince Pie

"Well, anyway, Mr. Qwilleran, I wanted to thank you and wish you a happy Thanksgiving . . . What are you going to do?" [asked Nancy Fincher]

"Polly Duncan is roasting a turkey, and there'll be another couple, and we'll all eat too much."

. . . It was a thankful foursome that gathered in Polly's apartment, thankful to be free after a week of confinement. The aroma of **turkey** was driving Bootsie to distraction, and the aroma of Mildred's **mince pie**, still warm from the oven, was having much the same effect on Qwilleran.

Polly carved the bird, pacifying Bootsie with some giblets, and the four sat down to the traditional feast.

Roast Turkey

8–12   pound turkey
⅓   cup butter or margarine, melted
2   teaspoons salt
½   cup all-purpose flour

Preheat oven to 325°. Wash turkey and remove any parts from inside body or neck cavity. Brush with melted butter or margarine and immediately rub with mixture of salt and flour, making a paste on the skin. Stuff turkey with dressing, if desired. Make a tent of aluminum foil and place it loosely over turkey to keep it from browning too rapidly. Bake 6–7 hours or until juices run clear and leg joint moves freely. Remove the foil the last 20 minutes so turkey can brown. Let stand 20 minutes before carving. SERVES 8–10.

Autumn Stuffing

½ cup chopped celery
¼ cup chopped onion
½ cup finely chopped carrot
¼ cup butter or margarine
½ teaspoon poultry seasoning
¼ teaspoon salt
⅛ teaspoon pepper
4 cups dry bread cubes
2 cups finely chopped peeled apple
¼ cup chopped pecans
¼ cup dried cranberries
¼ cup currants
⅓ cup chicken broth (approximate)

Sauté celery, onion, and carrot in butter or margarine until tender. Add poultry seasoning, salt, and pepper. Set aside. In a bowl, combine bread, apple, pecans, dried cranberries, and currants. Stir in sautéed vegetables. Sprinkle with enough chicken broth to moisten bread; toss. Place inside turkey cavity. SERVES 4–6.

NOTE: Recipe may be doubled or tripled depending on size of turkey and servings desired.

"Everyone had seconds of the bird and the squash puree with cashews."

Squash Puree

1 large peeled, and chopped butternut squash (about 5 cups)
½ cup chopped onion

¼ cup chopped celery
2 tablespoons butter or margarine
¼ cup chicken broth or stock
salt and pepper to taste
½ cup cashews, chopped

Place squash in a medium-sized saucepan; cover with water. Boil until tender. While squash is boiling, sauté the onion and celery in the butter or margarine. When squash is tender, drain and process in a food processor. Return squash to the saucepan; add the onion and celery, chicken broth or stock, salt, pepper, and cashews. Stir; simmer 10–15 minutes. SERVES 4–6.

Thanksgiving Potatoes

10 potatoes, peeled, and quartered
water for boiling potatoes
1 8-ounce package cream cheese, room temperature
1 cup sour cream
garlic powder to taste
milk, warmed
salt and pepper to taste
chives to taste
butter or margarine, melted

Preheat oven to 350°. Place potatoes in large saucepan; cover with salted water. Boil until soft; drain. While potatoes are boiling, mix cream cheese, sour cream, and garlic powder with electric mixer until smooth. Add hot potatoes slowly, beating well. Mix in milk, if desired, for a creamier consistency. Add salt, pepper, and chives. Place in baking dish. Brush top with melted butter or margarine. Bake for 30 minutes. SERVES 8–10.

Mildred's Mince Pie

Pastry:

- 2 cups all-purpose flour
- 1½ teaspoons salt
- ½ cup oil
- ½ cup cold milk

Mix flour and salt together. Add oil and half the milk to the flour. Stir with a fork. Add the rest of the milk a little at a time, if needed. Form dough into 2 balls. Roll each ball into a circle between 2 sheets of waxed paper. Remove one piece of waxed paper and place dough, paper side up, in an 8-inch pie pan. Remove paper. Reserve second circle of dough for top crust of pie.

Filling:

- 1 9-ounce package prepared mincemeat
- 1 cup water
- ¼ cup sugar
- 2 cups peeled, cored, chopped apples
- 1 tablespoon lemon juice

Set oven to 375°. In a saucepan, crumble mincemeat into small pieces. Add water and sugar. Bring to a boil. Drizzle apples with lemon juice. Add to mincemeat. Boil 3 minutes. Remove from heat and cool. Place cooled mincemeat mixture in pie pan lined with dough. Top with second circle of dough; crimp edges. Cut slits in top to release steam. Bake 40 minutes. SERVES 6.

À La Carte

Qwilleran pushed through the crowd to the dining room, where a caterer's long table was draped in a white cloth and laden with warming trays of **stuffed mushrooms**, *bacon-wrapped olives,* **cheese puffs**, *and other morsels too dainty for a hungry actor.*

Crab-Stuffed Mushrooms

24   large fresh mushrooms
1   6-ounce can flaked crabmeat
¼   cup fine dry bread crumbs
¼   cup sour cream
2   tablespoons butter or margarine, melted
2   tablespoons chopped green onions
1   tablespoon dry sherry (optional)
1   teaspoon Dijon mustard
paprika

Preheat oven to 425°. Remove stems from mushrooms and discard. Wash caps and place top-side down on a cookie sheet. Broil for 2 minutes. In a mixing bowl, combine crabmeat, bread crumbs, sour cream, butter or margarine, onions, sherry or equivalent amount of water, and Dijon mustard. Fill mushrooms with mixture. Sprinkle with paprika. Bake 8–10 minutes or until heated through. SERVES 12.

Starving Artist Cheese Puffs

———

1⅓ cups shredded cheddar cheese
1 tablespoon all-purpose flour
¼ teaspoon garlic powder
⅛ teaspoon salt
⅛ teaspoon pepper
3 egg whites, beaten until stiff
fine dry bread crumbs
oil

Mix the cheese, flour, garlic powder, salt, and pepper. Fold in the egg whites. Form small balls approximately 1 inch in diameter. Gently roll in bread crumbs. Deep fry in hot oil at 375° or fry in a skillet over medium-high heat. Drain on paper towels. Serve hot. SERVES 6–8.

"I have a new respect for potato farmers . . . and potatoes," he [Qwilleran] *said.*

A soft look suffused Nancy's face. "When Mom was alive, we used to dig down with our fingers and take out the small new tubers very carefully, so as not to interfere with the others. Then we'd have **creamed new potatoes with new peas.***"*

Creamed Potatoes and Peas

———

10-12 small new red potatoes
water for boiling potatoes
1 small clove garlic, minced

3 tablespoons butter or margarine
1 tablespoon all-purpose flour
2 cups half-and-half
salt and pepper to taste
1 cup new peas, cooked

Wash potatoes and boil in salted water until tender. Drain; set aside. In another pan, sauté garlic in butter or margarine. Add flour, stirring until well-mixed. Slowly add half-and-half, cooking until slightly thickened. Add additional salt, if desired, and pepper. Stir in peas and pour sauce over potatoes. Serve immediately. SERVES 4.

Pompously Qwilleran said, "I cannot tell a lie. I picked the lock of the library closet. There are tons of papers in there . . . There was also a recipe for Lena's angel food cake with chocolate frosting that sounded delicious."

"I knew Lena," said Junior. "She was Grandma's day-help for years and years."

Lena's Angel Food Cake

1½ teaspoons cream of tartar
½ teaspoon salt
1½ teaspoons vanilla extract
1½ cups egg whites (about 12) at room temperature
1 cup sugar
1 cup all-purpose flour
1¼ cups powdered sugar

Preheat oven to 375°. Add cream of tartar, salt, and vanilla extract to egg whites. Beat at high speed until very stiff, but still shiny. Beat in sugar, 2 tablespoonsful at a time. Continue to beat with mixer until meringue holds stiff peaks. Sift flour and powdered sugar together. Sift about ¼ of flour mixture over meringue and fold in lightly. Repeat until all flour mixture has been folded into egg whites. Place in ungreased 10-inch tube pan. Bake about 40 minutes. Invert pan and let cool before removing. Frost with chocolate frosting. Serves 10–12.

Chocolate frosting:
- 1   4-ounce package German sweet chocolate, broken into pieces
- 3   tablespoons butter
- 1½   cups powdered sugar
- 3   tablespoons hot water

In a small saucepan, melt chocolate and butter over low heat. Remove from heat. In a small bowl, mix together powdered sugar and hot water. Add the sugar mixture to the chocolate mixture. Stir well. Add more hot water, if necessary, to make frosting of pouring consistency. Pour over top of the cake.

The Cat Who Came to Breakfast

Qwilleran's friends, Nick and Lori Bamba, ask him to come to Breakfast Island to investigate incidents that are occurring. The "incidents" grow into "accidents" and then into murder. Koko gives Qwill clues by throwing catfits, raiding the nut bowl, and swishing dominoes here and there. Will Qwill interpret the clues?

Domino Inn
Double Breakfast

Eggs Benedict with Hollandaise Sauce

Johnnycakes

Country Maple Sausages

Lori's Apple Sauce

Qwilleran reported to the inn for his own breakfast with Penquin Island in one pocket of his waterproof jacket . . . . Parking his green-and-white umbrella on the porch, he went directly to the sunless sunroom. There were no other guests, and he was able to order both breakfasts without embarrassment: eggs Benedict with Hollandaise sauce and johnnycakes with sausages and apple sauce.

Eggs Benedict with Hollandaise Sauce

4 slices Canadian bacon
oil
1 tablespoon butter
2 English muffins, split
4 eggs

Fry bacon in oil. Butter muffins and toast them under broiler. Poach eggs to desired degree of doneness. Place bacon slices on muffins and eggs on bacon. Top with Hollandaise sauce. SERVES 4.

Hollandaise sauce:

2 egg yolks
1 tablespoon lemon juice
½ cup butter
⅛ teaspoon salt

Combine egg yolks, lemon juice, and ¼ cup butter in small saucepan. Cook over low heat, stirring constantly until butter melts. Add remaining butter and salt. Continue cooking, stirring constantly, until additional butter melts and sauce thickens. Serve hot. MAKES 1 CUP.

Johnnycakes

1 cup all-purpose flour
1 cup cornmeal
1 cup sugar
4 teaspoons baking powder
⅛ teaspoon salt
½ cup milk
1 egg, beaten
2 tablespoons butter or margarine, melted

Preheat oven to 400°. Mix flour, cornmeal, sugar, baking powder, and salt together. Mix milk, egg, and butter or margarine together; add to the flour mixture. Pour into 2 greased 8-inch cake pans. Bake 15 minutes. Cut into wedges. Serve while hot. SERVES 6–8.

Country Maple Sausages

1 7-ounce package fully cooked sausage links
2 tablespoons maple syrup
2 tablespoons brown sugar
1 tablespoon butter or margarine

Heat sausages according to package directions. Drain any excess water from skillet. Add maple syrup, brown sugar, and butter or margarine to sausages. Cook, stirring occasionally, on low heat for 5 minutes. SERVES 4.

Lori's Apple Sauce

4 cups peeled, cored, and chopped apples
⅓ cup brown sugar, packed
1 cup water
2 tablespoons butter or margarine
dash salt

Put the apples, sugar, water, butter or margarine, and salt into a saucepan. Simmer 1 hour, uncovered, stirring occasionally. SERVES 3–4.

À La Carte

It was quiet in the Corsair Room. The tables, most of them unoccupied, gleamed with white tablecloths, wineglasses, and flowers in crystal vases . . . The menu featured Creole and Cajun specialities, and he [Qwilleran] ordered a **gumbo** *described as an "incredibly delicious mélange of shrimp, turkey, rice, okra, and the essence of young sassafras leaves."*

Dwight said, "Okra! How can you eat that mucilaginous goo?"

"Are you aware that gumbo is the African word for okra?" Qwilleran asked with the lifted eyebrows of a connoisseur.

Gumbo

⅓   cup chopped onion

2   teaspoons oil

2   pounds sliced okra, fresh or frozen

1   6-ounce can tomato paste

½   cup chopped celery

⅓   cup chopped green peppers

4   cups water, boiling

¼   cup rice, uncooked

1½   pounds shrimp, cleaned

1½   cups turkey, cooked, diced

2   drops essence of sassafras

salt and pepper to taste

Sauté onion in oil in a saucepan. Add okra, tomato paste, celery, and green peppers, stirring constantly. Cook about 10 minutes. Slowly pour in boiling water. Stir in rice and simmer 30 minutes. Add shrimp, turkey, and more water, if needed. Season with sassafras, salt, and pepper. Simmer another 10 minutes. SERVES 6–8.

*". . . and the **cornbread** is right out of the oven."*

Cornbread

1 cup all-purpose flour
2 cups self-rising cornmeal
2 eggs, beaten
2 cups buttermilk
⅔ cup butter or margarine, melted

Preheat oven to 375°. Place a well-greased skillet, muffin pan, or corn stick pan in the oven to preheat. Mix the flour, cornmeal, eggs, and buttermilk. Stir well. Blend in the melted butter or margarine. Pour into heated pan. Bake 20–25 minutes. Serve while hot. SERVES 6–8.

For dessert Qwilleran ordered sweet potato pecan pie, which the waitress delivered with a rah-rah flourish . . .

Sweet Potato Pecan Pie

Pastry:

- ½ cup shortening
- 1½ cups all-purpose flour
- ½ teaspoon salt
- 3–4 tablespoons ice water

Cut the shortening into the flour and salt until the mixture resembles peas. Add the water a tablespoonful at a time, mixing lightly with a fork. When mixture holds together, gently press it into a ball. Roll out on a floured surface to about ¼ inch in thickness. Place in 9-inch pie pan.

Sweet potato pecan filling:

- 3 eggs, beaten
- 1 cup sweet potatoes, cooked, mashed
- 1 cup sugar
- 1 tablespoon all-purpose flour
- ½ cup corn syrup
- ½ teaspoon cinnamon
- ¼ teaspoon salt
- 1 cup pecans, chopped

Preheat oven to 350°. Mix the eggs, sweet potatoes, sugar, flour, corn syrup, cinnamon, and salt. Pour into unbaked pastry shell. Top with the pecans. Bake about 45 minutes or until toothpick inserted 2 inches from edge comes out clean. SERVES 6.

In the sunroom he nodded courteously to a few other guests and took a small table in a corner where he found a card [listing the menu] in Lori's handwriting:

Pecan Pancakes with Maple Syrup and *Turkey-apple Sausages* or *Tarragon-chive Omelette with Sautéed Chicken Livers*. . . .

"These pancakes are delicious," Qwilleran said to the plain-faced waitress, who shuffled about the sunroom.

Domino Inn Pecan Pancakes

1	cup all-purpose flour
1	tablespoon sugar
2	teaspoons baking powder
¼	teaspoon salt
1	egg, beaten
1	cup milk
1	tablespoon maple syrup
2	tablespoons vegetable oil
¼	cup + ¼ cup chopped pecans
	maple syrup

Mix the flour, sugar, baking powder, and salt. In another bowl combine egg, milk, syrup, and oil. Add liquids to the flour mixture. Stir lightly; batter will be lumpy. Add ¼ cup of the pecans. Pour batter by ¼ cupfuls onto a greased, heated griddle or skillet. Turn once when pancakes have a bubbly surface. Remove from skillet and place on plate in warm oven until all batter is used. Serve with additional maple syrup and remaining ¼ cup pecans. SERVES 4.

Turkey-Apple Sausages

½ cup fine, dry bread crumbs
½ cup peeled, cored, and finely chopped apple (Granny Smith)
1 pound turkey sausage

Mix bread crumbs and apple with sausage. Shape into patties. Fry until brown on both sides and pinkness is gone from the center of the patties. Serves 4–6.

Tarragon-Chive Omelette

---

4 eggs
¼ cup half-and-half
1 teaspoon dried tarragon
2 teaspoons dried chopped chives
salt and pepper to taste
2 teaspoons butter or margarine

Beat eggs and half-and-half until frothy. Add tarragon, chives, salt, and pepper. Heat butter or margarine in omelette pan or skillet. Pour in the egg mixture. Lift the edges of the eggs with a spatula, allowing the uncooked eggs to run underneath the cooked portion. When center is set, fold the bottom third of the omelette over and the top third up. Serves 2–3.

Mushroom Chicken Livers

---

1 pound chicken livers, cut into halves
¼ cup all-purpose flour
¼ cup butter or margarine

1   small onion, chopped
1   4-ounce can mushrooms, drained
salt and pepper to taste

Coat livers with flour. Heat butter or margarine in skillet. Sauté livers, onion, and mushrooms. Season with salt and pepper. Simmer 5 minutes or until tender. Drain on paper towel. SERVES 6.

He was going out to dinner, but it appeared that they needed the business, so he paid his money and took home a box that proved to contain a meatloaf sandwich, coleslaw, cookies, and . . . a pear!

Lunchbox Coleslaw

½   head cabbage, chopped
1   carrot, chopped
1   green pepper, chopped
1   onion, chopped
1–2   tablespoons sugar
salt and pepper to taste
mayonnaise

Shred vegetables in a food processor. Toss with sugar, salt, pepper, and enough mayonnaise to moisten. Cover and chill before serving. SERVES 4–6.

Brown Sugar Cookies

1 cup butter or shortening
2 cups brown sugar, packed
2 eggs
½ cup buttermilk
3½ cups all-purpose flour
1 teaspoon baking soda
1 teaspoon salt
1½ cups pecans

Cream butter or shortening and sugar. Add eggs and beat well. Add buttermilk; mix. Sift or mix flour, baking soda, and salt. Combine with sugar mixture. Add pecans. Chill 1 hour or more. Drop by rounded teaspoonsful onto greased cookie sheet. Bake 8–10 minutes at 400°. MAKES ABOUT 3 DOZEN COOKIES.

[Qwilleran] . . . *found Lori and asked if Harriet's Family Café would be open at that hour.* "All I want is some ice cream . . . Can you rustle up some chocolate ice cream with chocolate sauce?" [asked Qwilleran]

She [the cashier] *left the dining room and returned, saying,* "Vanilla is all."

"That'll do, if you have some *chocolate sauce*." [answered Qwilleran]

Late-Night Chocolate Sauce

4   squares semi-sweet chocolate
2   tablespoons butter
2   tablespoons milk
1   14-ounce can sweetened condensed milk
1   teaspoon vanilla extract

Melt the chocolate in top of a double boiler. Add butter, stir until melted. Slowly pour in the milk and sweetened condensed milk. Stir well. Remove from heat and add vanilla extract; stir. Serve over ice cream. Will keep 4–6 weeks refrigerated.

Writing the skit put Qwilleran in a good mood for an evening with the Rikers, and shortly before eight o'clock he called for a carriage and picked them up at their bed-and-breakfast . . .

The entrees were served. Qwilleran had recommended the Cajun menu, and all three had ordered pork chops étouffée.

"Why, these are nothing but smothered pork chops, highly seasoned," Riker said. "Mildred fixes these all the time."

Pork Chops Étouffée

4 tablespoons butter or margarine
2 teaspoons paprika
6 pork chops
Creole seasoning to taste
½ cup chopped onion
½ cup chopped green pepper
1 clove garlic, chopped
2 cups water
1 tablespoon Worcestershire sauce
salt to taste
2 tablespoons water
2 tablespoons cornstarch

Melt butter or margarine in a skillet and add paprika. Place pork chops in skillet and season with Creole seasoning. Brown chops and remove from skillet. Place onion, green pepper, and garlic in skillet; sauté. Return pork chops to skillet with vegetables. Add water, Worcestershire sauce, and salt. Simmer, covered, 45 minutes or until meat is tender. Add mixture of water and cornstarch to skillet. Stir gently until thickened. Serve with rice. SERVES 4–6.

Over dessert—the inevitable pecan pie—Mildred asked about the Siamese.

Pecan Pie

Pastry:

- ½ cup shortening
- 1½ cups all-purpose flour
- ½ teaspoon salt
- 3–4 tablespoons ice water

Cut the shortening into the flour and salt until the mixture resembles small peas. Add the water a tablespoonful at a time, mixing lightly with a fork. When mixture holds together, gently press into a ball. Roll it out on a floured surface to about ¼ inch in thickness. Place in 9-inch pie pan.

Pecan filling:

- 1 cup corn syrup
- 3 eggs, beaten
- 1 cup sugar
- 2 tablespoons butter, melted
- 1 teaspoon vanilla extract
- ⅛ teaspoon salt
- 1 cup pecans, chopped or halves

Preheat oven to 400°. Mix syrup, eggs, sugar, butter, vanilla extract, and salt. Stir well. Add pecans. Pour into unbaked pastry shell. Bake for 15 minutes. Reduce heat to 350° and bake 30 minutes or until outer edge of filling is firm and the center is slightly soft. SERVES 6.

*After **corned beef hash** with a poached egg, plus **hominy grits** with
sausage gravy (Lori was running out of ideas, he thought), he called the
number again.*

Corned Beef Hash

1 12-ounce can corned beef, broken up
4 medium potatoes, boiled and diced
1 small onion, chopped fine
2 tablespoons milk
salt and pepper to taste

Preheat oven to 350°. Combine all ingredients. Put into greased casserole dish. Bake 20 minutes. SERVES 4–6.

Hominy Grits

1½ cups grits
6 cups water
1½ sticks butter or margarine
1 pound shredded cheddar cheese
3 teaspoons salt
1 jalapeño pepper, chopped fine
3 eggs
1 cup water

Preheat oven to 300°. Cook grits as directed on package using 6 cups water. Add butter or margarine, cheese, salt, and jalapeño pepper to grits. Beat the eggs and add them plus the 1 cup water to grits. Mix well. Place in a greased baking dish. Bake 40–50 minutes. SERVES 4–6.

Sausage Gravy

1   pound ground sausage
3   tablespoons all-purpose flour
1½   cups water
1   cup milk
⅛   teaspoon garlic powder
½   teaspoon Worcestershire sauce

Break the sausage into small bits in a skillet. Cook, stirring occasionally, until pinkness is gone. Drain all but 3 tablespoonsful of the drippings. Add the flour to the warm sausage and drippings, stirring thoroughly. Mix the water, milk, garlic powder, and Worcestershire sauce together and slowly add it to the meat mixture, stirring constantly over low heat until gravy reaches desired consistency. SERVES 4.

Tea was served, and the conversation became general. The servers were two young men in green seersucker coats—island types but meticulously trained. There was tea with milk or lemon, and there was **pound cake.**

Pound Cake

---

3 cups sugar
1 stick butter or margarine
½ cup shortening
6 eggs
3 cups all-purpose flour
½ pint whipping cream
1 teaspoon vanilla extract

Preheat oven to 325°. Cream sugar, butter or margarine, and shortening. Beat in eggs. Add flour, whipping cream, and vanilla extract. Bake in greased, floured tube pan for 1½ hours. Cool 10 minutes in pan. Invert on wire rack and remove cake from pan. Cool completely. SERVES 8–10.

The Cat Who Blew the Whistle

Qwilleran and Polly, along with the other local dignitaries, take the first run of the old restored steam locomotive, the Lumbertown Party Train. They, nor anyone else, have any idea this may also be its last run. Soon there's the case of the missing millionaire and a murder for Qwill and Koko to solve.

Saturday Night Supper at the Palomino Paddock

She-Crab Soup

❖

Stuffed Mushrooms

❖

Paddock Caesar Salad

❖

Sea Scallops in Saffron Cream Sauce

❖

Grouper

In an effort to restore some of the magic, however, he proposed Saturday night dinner at the Palomino Paddock in Lockmaster, a five-star, five-thousand-calorie restaurant.

. . . When it was time to order from the menu, Qwilleran had no problem in making a choice: she-crab soup, an appetizer of mushrooms stuffed with spinach and goat cheese, a Caesar salad, and sea scallops with sun-dried tomatoes, basil, and saffron cream on angel hair pasta. Polly ordered grouper with no soup, no appetizer, and no salad.

She-Crab Soup

½   cup chopped onion
2   tablespoons butter or margarine
1   14½-ounce can diced tomatoes
2   8-ounce bottles clam juice
2   teaspoons lemon juice
⅛   teaspoon red pepper
¼   teaspoon dried thyme
¾   pound fresh crabmeat
½   cup cream
¼   cup sherry
½   teaspoon salt
⅛   teaspoon white pepper

Sauté onion in butter or margarine until translucent in a medium-sized saucepan. Add tomatoes, clam juice, lemon juice, red pepper, and thyme. Simmer 8–10 minutes. Cool slightly and place in blender; puree. Return to pan. Add crabmeat, cream, sherry, salt, and pepper. Heat through, but do not boil. SERVES 4.

Stuffed Mushrooms

12　large fresh mushrooms
1　tablespoon + 1 tablespoon butter or margarine, melted
¼　cup goat cheese
1　hard-boiled egg, finely chopped
¼　cup finely chopped fresh spinach
¼　cup finely diced water chestnuts
2　tablespoons dry bread crumbs

Cut off and discard ¼ inch of the bottom of the mushroom stems. Gently wash mushrooms and pat dry. Remove the remaining stems, chop, and set aside. Brush tops of mushrooms with 1 tablespoon of melted butter or margarine. Place cap side down in a greased baking dish. Broil in oven for one minute. While the mushroom caps are cooling, mix together cheese, egg, spinach, water chestnuts, 1 tablespoon butter or margarine, stems, and bread crumbs. Stuff mushroom caps with mixture. Broil in oven for two minutes or until heated through. SERVES 4–6.

Paddock Caesar Salad

1　clove garlic, crushed
½　cup olive oil
1　teaspoon salt
black pepper to taste
1　large lemon, juiced
1　egg, pasteurized, raw
2　heads romaine lettuce, torn into pieces, washed, and dried
6　anchovy fillets, mashed
½　cup fresh grated Parmesan cheese
2　cups croutons

Marinate garlic in olive oil for 24 hours. In a large salad bowl, combine salt, pepper, and lemon juice. Remove garlic from oil. Drizzle oil in bowl and blend with lemon mixture. Add egg and whip until slightly thickened. Add lettuce pieces and toss to coat. Sprinkle with anchovies, cheese, and croutons. SERVES 6–8.

Sea Scallops in Saffron Cream Sauce

2 tablespoons + 2 tablespoons butter or margarine
2 tablespoons finely chopped green onions
¼ cup chopped sun-dried tomatoes in oil, drained
1 pound sea scallops
1 cup whipping cream
3 tablespoons white wine
¼ teaspoon crushed or 2 strands saffron
½ teaspoon dried basil
salt to taste
white pepper to taste
angel hair pasta, cooked

Melt 2 tablespoons of the butter or margarine in a large skillet. Add onions and tomatoes; cook over medium-high heat for 3 minutes. Place in a small bowl and set aside. Melt 2 tablespoons butter or margarine. Add scallops and sauté until scallops are opaque—about 2 minutes.

Do not overcook. Remove scallops from pan, reserving the liquid. Add cream, wine, saffron, and basil to the skillet. Cook, stirring, over medium-high heat for 5 minutes. Add onion mixture, scallops, salt, and pepper. Heat through. Serve scallops and cream sauce over angel hair pasta. SERVES 4.

Grouper

1½ pounds grouper
salt and pepper to taste
2 tablespoons orange juice concentrate
2 tablespoons oil
⅛ teaspoon nutmeg

Preheat oven to 350°. Cut fish into 4 to 6 pieces. Season with salt and pepper. Grease a baking pan and place fish in pan. Mix orange juice concentrate, oil, and nutmeg. Spoon over fish. Cover and bake about 10 minutes or until fish is opaque and flakes with fork. Serves 2–4.

À La Carte

. . . He and Celia developed a chummy rapport. He called her [Celia Robinson] his secret agent, and she called him Chief. He sent her boxes of chocolate-covered cherries and the paperback spy novels that she liked; she sent him homemade brownies. They had never met.

Celia's Brownies

2 cups sugar
4 eggs

⅔   cup cooking oil

½   cup cocoa

1½   cups all-purpose flour

1   teaspoon baking powder

1   teaspoon salt

1   teaspoon vanilla extract

1   cup chopped nuts

Preheat oven to 350°. Add sugar to eggs and beat well. Mix oil and cocoa and add to egg mixture. Add flour, baking powder, salt, vanilla extract, and nuts. Pour into greased 9-inch by 13-inch pan. Bake approximately 35 minutes, being careful not to overbake. SERVES 8.

Qwilleran had reserved a table for four in the center of the dining car, where woodwork gleamed with varnish, tablecloths were blindingly white, and wineglasses sparkled . . . The soup course was served: jellied beef consommé. It was rather salty, according to Polly. The Chateaubriand *was an excellent cut of beef, and everyone agreed that neither the meat nor the chef could have come from Mudville . . . . By the time the* cheesecake *and coffee had been served, the train pulled into Flapjack.*

Chateaubriand

---

4   pounds tenderloin of beef

salt and pepper to taste

butter to cover tenderloin, room temperature

1   recipe Bernaise sauce

Preheat oven to 475°. Season meat with salt and pepper. Cover meat thickly with butter. Place in a roasting pan and put into the oven uncovered. Reduce the heat to 325°. Cook 20 to 30 minutes. Meat is cooked rare when it reaches 120° on a meat thermometer. Serve with Bernaise sauce. SERVES 8.

Bernaise sauce:

1	tablespoon finely chopped onion
½	cup white wine
1	teaspoon dried tarragon
2	crushed peppercorns
3	egg yolks
¾	cup butter, melted
¼	teaspoon salt

Boil the onion, wine, tarragon, and peppercorns until reduced to 2 tablespoons. Strain, reserving liquid, and allow to cool. In the top of a double boiler over barely simmering water, beat the egg yolks. Do not allow the water to touch the bottom of the pan. Add the butter a teaspoonful at a time, beating briskly the entire time. After all the butter has been added, stir in reserved wine mixture.

Cheesecake

Crust:

1¼	cups graham cracker crumbs
¼	cup sugar
¼	cup melted butter or margarine

Mix together and press on bottom and sides of 9-inch springform pan.

Filling:

- 5   8-ounce packages cream cheese, room temperature
- 1¾   cups sugar
- 3   tablespoons flour
- 6   eggs
- 3   teaspoons vanilla extract
- 1   teaspoon lemon juice
- ¼   cup cream

Preheat oven to 475°. Mix all ingredients until smooth and pour into crust. Bake 10 minutes at 475°. Reduce heat to 300° and bake an additional hour or until center is nearly firm.

Topping:

- 1   cup sour cream
- 3   tablespoons sugar
- ½   teaspoon vanilla extract

Increase oven temperature to 350°. Mix sour cream, sugar, and vanilla extract and spread on slightly cooled cake. Bake 5 minutes. Refrigerate until topping hardens. Remove sides from pan. Cake can be left on bottom of springform pan, cut, and placed on individual serving plates. SERVES 10–12.

*The train was rolling along at a comfortable excursion clip . . . The waiters kept pouring champagne, and Qwilleran produced a bag of **snacks** to accompany the drinks. "I'd like you to taste these," he said. "A friend of mine made them."*

Mildred, who wrote the food column for the newspaper, said they were actually croutons toasted with Parmesan cheese, garlic salt, red pepper, and Worcestershire sauce.

Kabibbles

---

day-old slices of bread
½ cup olive oil
1 teaspoon garlic salt
¼ teaspoon red pepper
1 tablespoon Worcestershire sauce
Parmesan cheese, grated

Preheat oven to 300°. Cut enough bread into ½-inch cubes to make 1 layer in a shallow roasting pan. Freeze before cutting if bread is too soft. Mix oil, garlic salt, pepper, and Worcestershire sauce thoroughly. Drizzle over the bread cubes and toss to coat evenly. Spread cubes over bottom of roasting pan. Sprinkle with cheese. Bake about 45 minutes or until brown and crisp. If not brown at end of hour, increase the temperature. SERVES 6.

"Where did you [Celia] have lunch?" [asked Qwilleran]

"Lois's Luncheonette, and Lois sent two free desserts to our table—bread pudding. It wasn't as good as mine. I use egg whites to make it fluffy and whole wheat flour to make it chewy, plus nuts and raisins, and vanilla sauce."

Celia's Better Bread Pudding

2 cups milk, scalded
3 slices whole wheat bread, torn into pieces
2 eggs, separated
½ cup sugar
⅛ teaspoon baking soda
1 teaspoon vanilla extract
½ cup chopped pecans
½ cup raisins

Preheat oven to 350°. Combine scalded milk and bread. Cool. Mix egg yolks, sugar, baking soda, vanilla extract, pecans, and raisins; add to milk/bread mixture. Fold in stiffly beaten egg whites. Place in greased baking dish. Put baking dish into a pan of water and bake 30–35 minutes. Top with vanilla sauce. SERVES 8.

Vanilla sauce:

1 tablespoon all-purpose flour
1 cup sugar
1 tablespoon butter or margarine, softened
2 egg yolks
1 cup boiling water
2 stiffly beaten egg whites
1 teaspoon vanilla extract

Mix flour with sugar in saucepan. Cream in butter or margarine and egg yolks. Add water. Cook over low heat, stirring, until thickened. Pour over stiffly beaten egg whites a small amount at a time, beating after each addition. Add vanilla extract. Serve over pudding.

When Celia arrived that evening, she flopped on the sofa, dropped her shapeless handbag on the floor, and said, "Could you put a little something in the lemonade tonight, Chief? I need it!"

"I mix a tolerable Tom Collins," he said. "I take it you've had a hectic day."

Tom Collins

2 ounces lemon juice
1 teaspoon sugar
2 ounces gin
cracked ice
club soda
lemon slice

Mix lemon juice, sugar, and gin in a highball glass. Add ice. Fill with club soda. Stir. Serve with lemon slice for garnish.

The Cat Who Said Cheese

Qwilleran is in his element! He's anticipating sampling the food, food, food that's everywhere with the opening of the Great Food Explo. There are designer pasties, dozens of soups, and even Scottish desserts. What Qwill doesn't anticipate is the murder of the hotel housekeeper.

Boulder House
Celebration Dinner

Amusing Trout

Serious Steak

Brussels Sprouts with Caraway

Spinach in Phyllo Pastry

Underhanded Turnip Soufflé

Zesty Sesame Seed Salad

Poached Pears

🐾

Polly was preparing to return to the workplace, half-days, and Qwilleran was taking her to Boulder House Inn in Trawnto for a celebratory dinner and overnight . . .

[The Boulder House] had been the summer residence of an eccentric quarry-owner, and it was constructed of rough boulders, some as big as bathtubs, piled one on another. In the dining room she [Polly] said she would have an **amusing piece of trout**. Qwilleran decided on a **serious steak**.

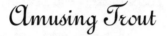

Amusing Trout

4   green onions
2   tablespoons butter or margarine
2   tablespoons fresh lemon juice
2   tablespoons fresh orange juice
1   tablespoon chopped fresh parsley
salt and pepper to taste
4   8-ounce trout, cleaned

Slice the white ends of the green onions very thin and sauté in the butter or margarine. Add lemon juice, orange juice, parsley, salt, and pepper. Place the trout in the skillet. Simmer, covered, until the thickest part of the trout turns opaque. Pour sauce from skillet over the trout when serving. SERVES 3–4.

Serious Steak

⅓ cup soy sauce
1 teaspoon ginger
2 cloves garlic, minced
⅓ cup Worcestershire sauce
¼ cup Burgundy wine
1 teaspoon lemon juice
½ teaspoon dry mustard
dash red pepper
4 T-bone steaks, 1½ to 2 inches thick

Mix all ingredients together thoroughly before placing steaks in marinade. Steaks can be left in the liquid and refrigerated overnight for a "serious" flavor or can be basted only as they are grilling for milder flavor. Grill or broil to desired degree of doneness. SERVES 4.

Accompanying the entrees were tiny brussels sprouts with caraway . . .

Brussels Sprouts with Caraway

2 10-ounce packages frozen or 1¼ pounds fresh brussels sprouts
water for boiling sprouts
1 tablespoon cornstarch
1 tablespoon water
1 tablespoon butter or margarine
1 tablespoon caraway seeds
salt and pepper to taste

Boil brussels sprouts in water until tender. Drain, reserving one cup of the liquid. Remove sprouts from pan and set aside. Mix cornstarch with 1 tablespoon water. Place reserved liquid back in saucepan. Add cornstarch mixture and stir over medium heat until slightly thickened. Stir in butter or margarine and caraway seeds. Return sprouts to pan. Season with salt and pepper. Stir to coat with sauce; heat sprouts through. SERVES 4–6.

. . . spinach and toasted almonds in phyllo pastry . . .

Spinach in Phyllo Pastry

1   16-ounce package phyllo pastry
½   cup almonds, sliced
1   teaspoon butter or margarine
⅛   teaspoon salt
1   10-ounce package frozen spinach, cooked, drained
½   cup mozzarella cheese
¼   cup bread crumbs
⅛   teaspoon dried basil
1   egg
1   tablespoon minced onion
½   cup butter or margarine, melted

Preheat oven to 400°. Thaw phyllo pastry according to package directions. Place almonds, butter or margarine, and salt on a small cookie sheet. Bake, stirring often until lightly browned. Remove from oven and reset temperature to 350°. Mix almonds with spinach, cheese, bread crumbs, basil, egg, and onion. Set aside. Place the 20 sheets of thawed phyllo dough on a cutting board. Have a damp cloth ready to cover the dough not being used. Cut dough into 3-inch by 14-inch strips. Layer 4 of the individual strips together, brushing with melted butter or margarine between each layer. Place one tablespoon of spinach mixture at the top of the strip. Fold corner over to make a triangle. Continue folding until strip is used. Brush ends with butter or margarine and tuck under triangle. Repeat layering, buttering, filling, and folding until all mixture is used. Bake for 25 minutes or until lightly browned. SERVES 6.

. . . and an *herb-flavored soufflé*, which Qwilleran pronounced excellent.

"*Of course, you know it's turnip,*" Polly informed him.

"*Well, they've done something to it—something underhanded,*" he said grudgingly.

Underhanded Turnip Soufflé

⅓   cup chopped onion
2   small cloves garlic, chopped
3   tablespoons butter or margarine
3   tablespoons all-purpose flour
1   cup milk
¾   cup shredded cheddar cheese
1   teaspoon dried dill weed
1   cup finely chopped cooked turnips
3   eggs yolks
salt and pepper to taste
3–4   egg whites

Preheat oven to 350°. Over medium-high heat, sauté onion and garlic in butter or margarine. Stir in the flour. Slowly add the milk, stirring constantly until thick. Add the cheese and dill weed. Stir until the cheese melts; add turnips. Remove from the heat and let cool. Separate the eggs. Beat the yolks. Add yolks to the cooled turnip mixture along with the salt and pepper. Beat the 3 egg whites until stiff. Add an extra egg white to make the soufflé lighter, if desired. Fold the egg whites into the turnip mixture. Pour into an ungreased 1½-quart soufflé dish. Bake for 30–40 minutes. Serve immediately. SERVES 4–6.

The salad course was *Bibb lettuce with lemon zest dressing and toasted sesame seeds*, garnished with a sliver of Brie.

"Don't eat your cheese," Qwilleran instructed Polly. "It's double-cream. I'll relieve you of it."

"That's so thoughtful of you, dear," she said.

Zesty Sesame Seed Salad

¼ cup cider vinegar
⅛ teaspoon pepper
⅛ teaspoon celery salt
¼ teaspoon dry mustard
3 teaspoons lemon juice
½ teaspoon lemon zest
½ cup sugar
¾ cup canola oil
4 teaspoons toasted sesame seeds
Bibb lettuce for 4
Brie cheese

Blend the vinegar, pepper, celery salt, dry mustard, lemon juice, and lemon zest in a blender. While blender is running, add sugar a teaspoonful at a time. Pour oil into mixture in a thin stream, continuing to blend at high speed. Place sesame seeds on cookie sheet. Broil for 5–8 minutes, until seeds are golden brown, stirring often. Serve lettuce with dressing and a sprinkle of toasted sesame seeds. Garnish with a sliver of Brie. SERVES 4.

Over dessert (poached pears stuffed with currants and pistachios and served with cherry coulis), Polly mentioned a subject that emphasized Qwilleran's predicament.

Poached Pears

4   ripe pears
4   teaspoons currants
4   teaspoons pistachio nuts, chopped
1   tablespoon lemon juice
3   cups water (approximate)
1   recipe cherry coulis

Peel and core pears, leaving the stem end closed. Mix the currants and pistachio nuts. Invert the pears and pour 2 teaspoons of the currants and nuts into the center of each pear. Combine the the lemon juice and water in a saucepan. Carefully place the pears, large end down, into the water and simmer gently for 5 minutes. Use a spatula to remove pears from water, keeping the pistachios and currants in place. Put a puddle of coulis in the middle of each plate. Place the pears upright in the coulis. Then pour a little more of the coulis over the pears. SERVES 4.

Cherry coulis:

1   12-ounce package frozen black cherries
1   cup + 2 tablespoons water
⅔   cup sugar
2   tablespoons cornstarch
2   tablespoons butter or margarine
¼   teaspoon ground ginger

Place cherries, 1 cup water, and sugar in a saucepan and bring to a boil. Lower the heat and simmer 5 minutes. Let cool slightly and puree in a blender. Return mixture to the saucepan. Mix the cornstarch and 2 tablespoons water; add it to the cherry mixture. Add the butter or margarine and stir over medium heat until thick and bubbly. Blend in the ginger and boil one more minute.

À La Carte

Having worked against odds, the writer of the "Qwill Pen" finished in time for the meeting at the newspaper office. He [Qwilleran] walked first to Lois's Luncheonette for a piece of **apple pie***.*

. . . Qwilleran, always entertained by Lois's discourses, arrived at the newspaper conference in good humor.

Lois's Apple Pie

Pastry:
    ½   cup shortening
    1½   cups all-purpose flour
    ½   teaspoon salt
    3–4 tablespoons ice water

Cut the shortening into the flour and salt until the mixture resembles small peas. Add the water a tablespoonful at a time, mixing lightly with a fork. When mixture holds together, gently press into a ball and then roll it out on a floured surface to about ¼ inch in thickness. Place in 9-inch pie pan.

Apple filling:

- ½ cup sugar
- ½ cup brown sugar, packed
- 1 tablespoon all-purpose flour
- ½ teaspoon salt
- ½ teaspoon cinnamon
- ½ teaspoon nutmeg
- 5 cups peeled, cored, and sliced cooking apples

Preheat oven to 425°. Mix together sugars, flour, salt, cinnamon, and nutmeg. Add apples. Toss gently to coat apples with sugar mixture. Place apples in an unbaked pastry shell. Sprinkle with topping. Bake 15 minutes; reduce heat to 350° and bake 45 minutes longer. SERVES 6.

Topping:

- ¾ cup all-purpose flour
- ½ cup brown sugar, packed
- ⅓ cup butter or margarine
- ⅓ cup chopped walnuts

Blend flour with brown sugar and butter or margarine until crumbly. Add nuts.

"Guess who visited me today and brought some gourmet **mushroom soup**! *Elaine Fetter!"* [said Polly]

. . . *"How was the soup?"* [asked Qwilleran]

"Delicious, but too rich for my diet . . . Incidentally, she grows her own mushrooms—shiitake, no less."

Elaine's Cream of Mushroom Soup

----

4 cups of a variety of sliced mushrooms—button, shiitake, and portobello, cleaned and sliced
1 tablespoon + 3 tablespoons butter or margarine
3 tablespoons all-purpose flour
¼ teaspoon dried thyme
1 14½-ounce can chicken broth or chicken stock
1 cup light cream
salt and pepper to taste

Sauté mushrooms 5 minutes over medium heat with 1 tablespoon butter or margarine. Set aside. In a medium saucepan melt remaining butter or margarine. Stir in flour and thyme. Add broth and cook until slightly thickened. Add mushrooms, cream, salt, and pepper. Cook and stir until heated through. SERVES 4.

The Great Food Explo was about to blast off . . . Friday was the big day in Pickax . . . At 11:00 A.M. the public started to gather for the noon ribbon-cutting . . . What he [Qwilleran] saw was a row of seven new business enterprises . . . They were: . . . The Spoonery, dedicated to fast-feeding with a spoon, either at a sit-down counter or a stand-up bar. Opening day specials: sausage gumbo, butternut squash soup with garlic and cashews, borscht, and tomato-rice.

Sausage Gumbo

½ cup chopped onion

1 cup chopped green pepper

1 pound Polish sausage, sliced in ¼-inch slices

1 tablespoon vegetable oil

1 16½-ounce can diced tomatoes

1 6-ounce can tomato juice

2 cups frozen cut okra

2 cups water

½ cup white rice, uncooked

salt and pepper to taste

Cook onion, green pepper, and sausage in oil in a large skillet. Drain off fat. Add tomatoes and tomato juice. Cook and stir till bubbly. Add okra. Simmer for 10 minutes. Add water and rice. Bring to a boil. Stir; reduce heat and simmer, covered, for 20 minutes or until rice is tender. Season with salt and pepper. Use additional water while simmering, if necessary. SERVES 6.

Butternut Squash Soup

1½ cups chopped cooked butternut squash

1 14½-ounce can chicken broth

2 tablespoons butter or margarine

1 tablespoon all-purpose flour

¼ teaspoon ground ginger

½ teaspoon minced garlic

1 cup half-and-half

½ cup salted cashews, finely chopped

salt and pepper to taste

In a blender or food processor, puree squash and ¾ cup of the chicken broth. Set aside. Melt butter or margarine in a saucepan. Add flour, ginger, and garlic. Stir thoroughly. Slowly pour in half-and-half. Cook until slightly thickened, stirring constantly. Add squash puree, remaining broth, cashews, salt, and pepper. Cook until heated through. Garnish with additional cashews, if desired. SERVES 4.

Borscht

1	pound fresh beets, washed and trimmed of roots and stems
2	medium carrots, chopped
1	large stalk celery, chopped
1	medium-sized onion, chopped
½	cup shredded cabbage
1	clove garlic, minced
1	14½-ounce can beef broth
½	cup water
2	teaspoons brown sugar
¼	teaspoon dried dill weed
⅛	teaspoon celery salt
½	teaspoon caraway seeds (optional)
	salt and pepper to taste
½	cup sour cream
1	tablespoon fresh parsley, chopped

Boil beets about 10 minutes so they will peel more easily. Peel the beets; chop and place them in a saucepan with the carrots, celery, onion, cabbage, and garlic. Add the broth, water, sugar, dill weed, and celery salt. Bring mixture to a boil. Reduce heat and simmer, covered, for about 40 minutes or until vegetables are tender. For a thicker soup, puree half of the mixture and return it to the pan with the remaining soup. If desired, the entire mixture can be pureed. Add additional salt, if desired, and pepper. Place a dollop of sour cream on individual servings of soup, then sprinkle with parsley. SERVES 4.

Tomato and Rice Soup

½   cup chopped celery
½   cup chopped onion
2   cloves garlic, minced
1   medium tomato, chopped
3   tablespoons butter or margarine
2   14½-ounce cans chicken broth
1   15-ounce can tomato sauce
½   teaspoon sugar
½   teaspoon dried basil
¼   teaspoon dried parsley
¼   cup rice, uncooked
salt and pepper to taste

Sauté the celery, onion, garlic, and tomato in the butter or margarine. Add the broth, tomato sauce, sugar, basil, and parsley. Simmer, covered, for about 10 minutes. Strain the mixture, discarding the vegetables. Add the rice to the remaining tomato liquid. Add salt and pepper. Simmer, covered, until the rice is cooked. SERVES 4–6.

"A bunch of students will be coming from the college to help serve, pick up empties, and all that."

"And what kind of punch are you serving?"

"None of your sissy-pink punches," said Jerry Sip. "The **non-alky bowl** will have three kinds of fruit juices plus a slug of strong cold tea and a dash of bitters. With the tea and the cranberry juice, it'll have a good color."

Non-alky Punch

4 quarts water
3 cups sugar
2 6-ounce cans frozen lemon juice
1 quart orange juice
1 pint cranberry juice
1 pint strong tea
dash bitters

Mix water and sugar in a saucepan. Bring to a boil. Combine with remaining ingredients; stir thoroughly. Chill. MAKES 2 GALLONS.

*"I don't imagine Iris ever put her name on it [her cookbook]. If she did, no doubt it's been obliterated. But first you should look for almost illegible handwriting. Next you might look for certain recipes that made her a legend in her time, like butter pecan gingersnaps and lemon coconut squares. She also had a secret way with **meat loaf** and macaroni and cheese."*

Mrs. Cobb's Meat loaf

1½   tablespoons brown sugar, packed
½ cranberry sauce (Mrs. Cobb's secret ingredient)
2   eggs
3   tablespoons finely chopped onion
½   cup milk
¼   teaspoon ground thyme
⅛   teaspoon sage
dash nutmeg
1   teaspoon salt
¼   teaspoon pepper
⅔   cup plain dry bread crumbs
1½   pounds extra-lean ground beef

Preheat oven to 350°. Stir brown sugar and cranberry sauce together until smooth. Place in bottom of 9-inch by 5-inch loaf pan. In a bowl, combine eggs, onion, milk, thyme, sage, nutmeg, salt, and pepper. Stir in bread crumbs. Add ground beef and mix thoroughly. Shape into a loaf and place on top of cranberry mixture. Flatten top so loaf will sit level when inverted. Bake 1 hour and 15 minutes. Let sit 10 minutes; invert on plate and serve. SERVES 4–6.

The Cat Who Tailed a Thief

The unthinkable is happening! Pickax is experiencing "big-city" crimes. A wave of thievery is taking place. Next, the banker is murdered. Then someone is poisoned and Qwill, Koko, and Yum Yum step in to bring the guilty parties to justice.

Onoosh's Mediterranean Supper

Hummus with Warm Pita

Lentil Soup

Tabbouleh

Shish Kebob

Stuffed Grape Leaves

Spicy Walnut Cake

Tonight, Qwilleran took one last look in the full-length mirror, said good-bye to two bemused animals, and drove to Onoosh's Mediterranean Café in downtown Pickax . . . Qwilleran had not tried the restaurant before suggesting it to the banker. When he arrived, he felt transported halfway around the globe by the aroma of strange spices and the twang of ethnic music. Two waitpersons were hurrying about, wearing European farmer smocks but looking like students from the community college.

He [Willard Carmichael, the banker] ordered **hummus** *and asked to have the* **pita** *served warm.*

Hummus

---

1   19-ounce can garbanzo beans (chickpeas)
¼   cup tahini (sesame-seed paste—available at most health food stores)
3   tablespoons lemon juice
2   cloves garlic, chopped
¼   teaspoon cumin
¼   teaspoon salt
¼   teaspoon pepper
pita bread, cut into wedges

Drain garbanzo beans, reserving liquid. Place garbanzos, tahini, lemon juice, garlic, cumin, salt, pepper, and ¼ cup of the reserved liquid in a food processor or blender. Process until smooth and the consistency of thick cream. Add more liquid, if necessary. Serve with warm pita bread. MAKES 1½ CUPS.

Their dinner orders were taken, and both men chose the lentil soup . . .

Lentil Soup

2   onions, chopped
oil
⅓   cup tomato paste
5   cups water
2   cups lentils, rinsed and sorted
jalapeño pepper to taste, chopped
½   teaspoon salt
limes, cut into wedges

Sauté onions in oil in a medium-sized saucepan. Stir in tomato paste and ½ cup of the water. Cook, stirring, for about 5 minutes. Add the rest of the water, lentils, jalapeño pepper, and salt. Bring to a boil. Reduce heat and simmer, covered, about 45 minutes. Stir occasionally. Add additional water, if necessary. Serve with lime wedges to squeeze over soup. SERVES 6–8.

. . . with tabbouleh as the salad course . . .

Tabbouleh

1   cup bulgur wheat
1½   cups boiling water
1   teaspoon salt
¼   cup lemon juice
¼   cup olive oil

⅓ cup finely chopped fresh mint leaves or 2 tablespoons dried mint
1 bunch green onions, chopped
⅓ cup chopped fresh parsley or 2 tablespoons dried parsley
1 large tomato, chopped

Mix bulgur wheat and boiling water. Cover and let stand for 30 minutes. Add the rest of the ingredients except the tomato. Mix well. Chill several hours. Add tomato just before serving. SERVES 2–4.

. . . followed by shish kebob for Will and stuffed grape leaves for Qwill.

Shish Kebob

⅓ cup lemon juice
2 tablespoons oil
½ teaspoon salt
¼ teaspoon pepper
½ teaspoon oregano
1 pound boneless lamb, cut into 1-inch cubes
1 green pepper cut into small pieces
1 onion, cut into small pieces
1 cup cubed eggplant
skewers

Make marinade of lemon juice, oil, salt, pepper, and oregano. Add lamb and marinate 6–8 hours or overnight in refrigerator. Remove lamb, reserving marinade, and skewer with the green pepper, onion, and eggplant. Brush green pepper, onion, and eggplant with reserved marinade; discard remaining marinade. Broil shish kebobs in oven or on grill 5–8 minutes on each side or until meat has reached desired degree of doneness. SERVES 4.

Qwilleran . . . said to the server, "Would you ask Onoosh if she can make *meatballs in little green kimonos?*"

In less than a minute she came rushing from the kitchen in her white apron and chef's toque. "Mr. Qwill!" she squealed. "It's you! I knowed it was you!"

Stuffed Grape Leaves

1 pound ground lamb
1 cup cooked rice
2 onions, finely chopped
1½ teaspoons salt
¼ teaspoon pepper
2 tablespoons dried mint or ⅓ cup finely chopped fresh mint
1 1-pound jar grape leaves in vinegar brine
1 14½-ounce can chicken broth

Combine the lamb, rice, onions, salt, pepper, and mint in a bowl. Mix well. Place the mixture, by tablespoonful, on the ribbed side of the grape leaves. Roll the leaves, tucking in the sides. Place stuffed leaves side by side in a large skillet. Cover with chicken broth. Bring to a boil. Then lower the temperature and cook over low heat 50–60 minutes or until rice is tender and meat is cooked. Add water while cooking, if necessary. SERVES 6–8.

They ordered spicy walnut cake and dark-roast coffee.

Spicy Walnut Cake

1½ cups chopped walnuts
½ tablespoon + 2 cups all-purpose flour
1 cup oil
1 cup sugar
1 teaspoon baking soda
1 teaspoon baking powder
1 teaspoon salt
1 tablespoon ground cinnamon
¼ teaspoon nutmeg
¼ teaspoon ground cloves
½ teaspoon ground ginger
1 cup buttermilk

Preheat oven to 350°. Place walnuts and ½ tablespoon flour in plastic bag. Shake until walnuts are well-coated. Set aside. Mix oil and sugar. Sift or mix together the 2 cups flour, baking soda, baking powder, salt, cinnamon, nutmeg, cloves, and ginger. Combine with the sugar mixture, alternating with the buttermilk. Gently fold in floured walnuts. Pour into greased and floured 9-inch by 13-inch pan. Bake for 30 minutes. Pour topping over cake as soon as taken from oven. SERVES 15.

Topping:
½ cup sugar
½ cup buttermilk
3 tablespoons butter or margarine
1 tablespoon corn syrup
½ teaspoon baking soda

Place sugar, buttermilk, butter or margarine, and corn syrup in a saucepan. Stirring constantly, bring to a boil over high heat. Lower heat and continue to boil, stirring, for 5 minutes. Remove from heat and add baking soda; stir and pour over cake immediately.

À La Carte

There was a Scotch pine tree in the living room, trimmed like the one at their [the Rikers'] wedding the previous Christmas: white pearlescent ornaments, white doves, white streamers. The aromas were those of pine boughs, roasting turkey, and **hot mulled cider.** *Polly said, "I always feel so secure when I come to dinner here. Mildred doesn't fuss in the kitchen; she doesn't expect anyone to help; and everything turns out perfectly: the hot foods hot and the cold foods cold."*

Toulouse walked into the room with a solemn tread and rubbed against the cook's ankles as a reminder that the turkey was ready. Mildred served it with a **brown-rice-and-walnut stuffing, twice-baked sweet potatoes with orange glaze,** *sesame-sauced broccoli, and* **two kinds of cranberry relish.**

Hot Mulled Cider

---

3 quarts apple juice
1½ teaspoons whole cloves
1½ teaspoons whole allspice
3 sticks cinnamon
1 cup brown sugar, packed
¾ teaspoon salt

Combine all ingredients in saucepan. Slowly bring to a simmer. Cover and continue to simmer for 10 minutes. Remove spices with slotted spoon. Serve hot. (Spices can be placed in small cloth bag before adding to cider for easy removal.) SERVES 12.

Brown-Rice-and-Walnut Stuffing

---

3 cups brown rice
2 tablespoons butter or margarine
½ cup chopped celery
¼ cup chopped onion
½ teaspoon poultry seasoning
½ cup chopped walnuts

Cook rice according to package directions. In another saucepan, melt the butter or margarine. Add the celery and onion and sauté until vegetables are tender. Add poultry seasoning, celery, onion, and walnuts to rice. Place inside rinsed cavity of turkey. May be doubled or tripled depending upon turkey size. SERVES 6.

Twice-Baked Sweet Potatoes

---

4   sweet potatoes
3   tablespoons butter or margarine, melted
2   tablespoons brown sugar, packed
1   8-ounce can crushed pineapple, drained
⅓   cup chopped pecans

Preheat oven to 375°. Bake the potatoes until tender. Cut in half, lengthwise, and scoop out the potato pulp. Leave enough pulp in potato shell so that shell will hold its shape. Mix pulp with the butter or margarine, brown sugar, pineapple, and pecans. Put the mixture back into the potato shells. Bake until heated through. Serve with orange glaze. SERVES 4–6

Orange glaze:
1   tablespoon cornstarch
1   cup orange juice
1   tablespoon sugar
1   tablespoon butter or margarine

Mix cornstarch with a little orange juice. Place remainder of orange juice in a small saucepan. Add the cornstarch mixture to the orange juice. Stir in sugar and butter or margarine. Cook, stirring constantly, until thickened.

"I feel compelled to serve two kinds" [of cranberry relish] *she said, "or the turkey will be dry and the stuffing will be soggy. It's just a superstition."*

Mildred's #1 Cranberry Relish Salad

1   3-ounce box raspberry gelatin
1   cup boiling water
1   16-ounce can whole cranberry sauce
½   cup chopped nuts
1   cup sour cream

Dissolve gelatin in water. Chill until slightly thickened. Stir cranberry sauce to soften and fold into the thickened gelatin. Add nuts. Place mixture in pan and swirl in the sour cream. Chill until firm. SERVES 6.

Mildred's #2 Cranberry Relish Salad

4   oranges, seeded
2   pounds fresh cranberries
4   unpeeled apples, cored
4   cups sugar
1   cup chopped walnuts

Peel rind from oranges. Remove and discard white membranes. Grind orange peeling, orange pulp, cranberries, and apples in food grinder. Add sugar and walnuts. Mix well. Chill several hours covered. SERVES 6–8.

The dietician at the hospital had given her [Polly] seventeen low-calorie, low-cholesterol recipes for glamorizing a flattened chicken breast: with lemon and toasted almonds, with artichoke hearts and garlic, and so forth. "Think of it as scaloppine di pollo appetito," Polly suggested.

Scaloppine Di Pollo Appetito

2   chicken breasts, flattened to between ¼ and ½ inch in thickness
½   teaspoon grated lemon peel
¼   cup fresh or bottled lemon juice
1   tablespoon canola oil
2   tablespoons finely chopped onion
1   teaspoon sugar
½   teaspoon Worcestershire sauce
¼   teaspoon dry mustard
¼   teaspoon salt
¼   teaspoon pepper
2   tablespoons sliced almonds

Place chicken breasts in a flat, shallow bowl. In another bowl, combine lemon peel, lemon juice, oil, onion, sugar, Worcestershire sauce, mustard, salt, and pepper to make a marinade. Pour over chicken, turning chicken to make sure marinade coats both sides, and cover. Refrigerate about 1 hour. Place chicken on broiler rack sprayed with no-stick cooking spray or lightly greased. Place rack in broiler pan, brush chicken with additional marinade. Discard remaining marinade and broil, about 3–4 minutes, on each side or until white in center. Sprinkle with almonds about 1 minute before chicken is done to toast almonds. SERVES 2.

"It's Scottish Night! You're going to wear your kilt. I wish I could see you before you leave. What time is the dinner?" [asked Polly]

"I leave at six-thirty, with trepidation," he [Qwilleran] *admitted . . .*

Then dinner was served: Forfar bridies, taters and neeps, *and Pitlochry salad.*

Forfar Bridies

Pastry:

½	cup butter or margarine
½	cup lard
4	cups all-purpose flour
½	teaspoon salt
10–12	tablespoons ice water

Cut butter or margarine and lard into flour and salt with pastry blender or fork. Add water a little at a time, mixing lightly with fork. When dough clings together, form into ball. Divide dough into 3 sections.

Filling:

½	pound ground sirloin or chuck
½	teaspoon salt
½	teaspoon pepper
½	cup chopped onion
¼	teaspoon dry mustard
¼	cup beef broth

Preheat oven to 375°. Mix all ingredients together thoroughly. Roll out one section of dough to ¼-inch in thickness. Cut into 4-inch circles. Place a teaspoonful of the filling on the bottom half of each circle. Moisten the top edge of dough; fold down over meat filling and crimp edges with fork. Make two holes in center with a skewer indicating that it is filled with meat and onion. (One hole is used when the filling is meat only.) Repeat with remaining dough and filling. Bake on ungreased cookie sheet 35 minutes. MAKES 3 DOZEN BRIDIES.

Taters and Neeps

2   cups diced potatoes
2   cups diced turnips
1   teaspoon salt
¼   teaspoon white pepper
2   egg whites
1   recipe white sauce

White sauce:

2   tablespoons butter or margarine
1   tablespoon cornstarch
1¼   cups half-and-half
½   teaspoon salt
⅛   teaspoon white pepper
1   hard-boiled egg, finely chopped

Preheat oven to 350°. Boil potatoes and turnips together until tender. Drain and mash. Season with salt and pepper. Let cool while beating egg whites until stiff peaks form. Fold into potatoes and turnips. Put in buttered casserole dish and bake uncovered 40–45 minutes. While baking, prepare white sauce by melting the butter or margarine in a saucepan. Blend in cornstarch. Add half-and-half and cook over low heat, stirring constantly until thick and smooth. Add salt, pepper, and egg to sauce. Serve over warm potato and turnip casserole. SERVES 4.

While dressing to have dinner at Polly's (flattened chicken breast with ripe olives, garbanzos, and sun-dried tomatoes), Qwilleran received another annoying phone call from Danielle . . . After dinner—it was the best [chicken] recipe so far—they listened to the tapes Qwilleran had recorded for Tall Tales.

Polly's Chicken

2 tablespoons olive oil

½ cup sun-dried tomatoes in oil, drained, cut into thin strips

1 clove garlic, chopped

¼ cup finely chopped onion

4 boneless, skinless chicken breasts, flattened

1 14½-ounce can chicken broth

salt and pepper to taste

juice of ½ lemon

12 ripe olives, chopped

1 19-ounce can garbanzo beans (chickpeas)

Heat oil in a large skillet and sauté tomatoes, garlic, and onion until onion is tender. Push tomato mixture to one side of skillet. Add the chicken and cook about 5 minutes on each side. Add broth and simmer 15 minutes before adding salt, pepper, lemon juice, and olives. Simmer until chicken is tender. Pour tomato mixture over warmed garbanzo beans when served. SERVES 4.

The Cat Who Sang for the Birds

Spring is in the air, but that's not all that's in the air. Someone is spray-painting graffiti on a barn, someone is stealing pictures from the Art Center, a young artist disappears, and Widow Coggin loses her life in a fire at her farm. It falls to Qwilleran to find out who is responsible. Koko tries hard to help Qwill. Will Qwilleran be able to understand the clues?

Brunch in the Apple Barn

Fruit Soup

Mushroom Frittata

Asparagus and Yellow Pepper Salad

Before attending the grand opening of the Art Center, four friends met for Sunday brunch at Qwilleran's barn . . . Brunch preliminaries were held in the gazebo, where the screened panels on all eight sides gave the impression of being pleasantly lost in the woods. The foursome pulled chairs into a semicircle overlooking the bird garden: the Siamese sat complacently at their feet, watching the crows, mourning doves, and blue jays . . .

"What's bugging him?" [Koko] Arch asked.

"He knows the dinnerbell is about to ring." [answered Qwilleran] . . .

The dinnerbell that had summoned them was standing on the console table in the foyer—a cast brass handbell with a coiled serpent for a handle . . . Brunch was served in the dining area, which was seldom used; guests were always taken out to dinner.

It began with **fruit soup**, *a concoction of pear and raspberry.*

Fruit Soup

1   cup water
¾   cup sugar
3   cups fresh raspberries
2   pears, very ripe, cored, peeled, and chopped
1½   tablespoons cornstarch
3   tablespoons water
sour cream

Bring the water and sugar to a boil. Add the berries. Boil for about 1 minute. Strain to remove the seeds. Puree the pears in a food processor or blender with the strained raspberry liquid. Return to pan and boil 1 more minute. Mix the cornstarch and water and add to the fruit mixture. Cook, stirring constantly, until thickened. Can be served hot or cold. Garnish with a dollop of sour cream before serving. SERVES 4.

*Then came **mushroom frittata** . . . If Qwilleran had not later found two small yellow cartons in the trash container, he would never have guessed the eggs in the frittata were cholesterol-free.*

Mushroom Frittata

½   pound fresh sliced mushrooms
⅓   cup chopped onion
1   tablespoon olive oil
½   cup sour cream
2   8-ounce cartons egg substitute or 8 eggs
¼   teaspoon dried basil
salt and pepper to taste

Preheat oven to 350°. Sauté the mushrooms and onion in olive oil. In a small bowl, mix the sour cream, egg substitute or eggs, basil, salt, and pepper. Add the vegetable mixture to the egg mixture. Pour into a greased baking dish and bake 10–12 minutes or until almost set in the center. SERVES 4.

. . . and a warm salad of **asparagus and yellow peppers.**

Asparagus and Yellow Pepper Salad

Dressing:

½ cup oil
⅓ cup sugar
⅓ cup white vinegar
1 tablespoon chopped fresh chives
1 teaspoon chopped fresh dill weed
1 teaspoon dried tarragon
salt and pepper to taste

Mix all ingredients and bring to a boil in a small saucepan. Then lower the heat and simmer until the sugar is dissolved, stirring frequently. Cool slightly before pouring over the vegetables. SERVES 4.

Vegetables for salad:

1 pound asparagus
1 red onion, sliced
1 yellow pepper, sliced

Steam the asparagus, onion, and pepper to desired degree of tenderness. Pour the slightly cooled dressing over the vegetables and serve warm.

À La Carte

. . . The front door was flung open, and a scrawny woman in strange cloth-ing screeched, "Who be you?"

Qwilleran raised the bakery box and replied in a pleasant voice, "A messenger from the Moose County Something, *bringing a present to one of our favorite readers! . . . I hope you like these* **muffins**, *Mrs. Coggin. They're* **carrot and raisin**."

Carrot Raisin Muffins

2 cups + 2 teaspoons all-purpose flour
1 teaspoon baking soda
1 teaspoon baking powder
2 teaspoons cinnamon
2 cups sugar
½ teaspoon salt
½ cup raisins
½ cup flaked coconut
1 cup oil
2 teaspoons vanilla extract
2 cups grated raw carrots
4 eggs, slightly beaten
½ cup chopped pecans
cream cheese (optional)

Preheat oven to 350°. Sift or mix the 2 cups flour, baking soda, baking powder, cinnamon, sugar, and salt together. Add raisins and coconut. Combine the dry-ingredient mixture with the oil, vanilla extract, carrots, and eggs. Mix well. Place pecans in a plastic bag with 2 teaspoons flour. Shake to cover pecans evenly to help prevent them from sinking to the bottom of the batter. Add pecans to batter; divide batter evenly among 24 medium-sized greased or papered muffin tins. Bake 25 minutes or until toothpick inserted in center of muffin comes out clean. Cool a few minutes, then remove from pans. Serve with cream cheese, if desired. MAKES 24 MUFFINS.

Qwilleran, dressed in grubbies for his dinner date at Chet's Bar &
Barbecue, watched them [his Siamese] gobble their canned crabmeat
garnished with goat cheese . . .

When Qwilleran entered Chet's for the first time, all the tables were
filled, and the atmosphere was hazy with smoke. Wetherby Goode signaled
him from the bar . . .

An overworked waitress interrupted. "Pork, beef, or turkey? Sandwich
or platter? Hot-mild, hot-hot, or call 911?" In a matter of seconds she
was back with plastic plates piled high, while two fluffy white rolls teetered
on the summit.

Hot-Mild Barbecued Beef

3–4 pound round bottom roast
water
1 cup chopped onion
2 tablespoons oil
2 teaspoons paprika
1 teaspoon dry mustard
1 tablespoon vinegar
3 tablespoons Worcestershire sauce
1 teaspoon pepper
1 teaspoon salt
cayenne pepper to taste
3 tablespoons brown sugar, packed

1   large clove garlic, chopped
1   16-ounce can tomato paste
1   teaspoon molasses
¼   cup ketchup

Bake roast, covered, in pan filled ¼ full of water, approximately 4 hours or until fork tender. In a large pot, sauté onion in oil. Add remaining ingredients. Simmer for 20–30 minutes. Remove meat from pan and shred into small pieces. Add the meat to the sauce and mix well. Cook, covered, over low heat for about 30 minutes. Add more water, if necessary. SERVES 8–10.

A Saturday night dinner at the Palomino Paddock would be a special occasion on anyone's calendar, and Polly—for her date with Qwilleran— wore her pink silk suit and opal jewelry . . .

There were no prices on Polly's menu, but they were known to be $$$$$ in the restaurant ratings, meaning extra-expensive. The evening's special was tenderloin of ostrich with smoked tomatoes, herbed polenta, and black currant coulis . . . She ordered a vegetarian curry. Qwilleran took a chance on the big bird, medium rare.

Herbed Polenta

2 small cloves garlic, minced
½ cup finely chopped onion
2 tablespoons oil
¼ teaspoon basil
¼ teaspoon tarragon
4 cups chicken stock
2 teaspoons butter
1 cup yellow cornmeal
¼ cup shredded cheddar cheese
salt and pepper to taste

Preheat oven to 350°. Sauté garlic and onion in the oil. Add basil and tarragon. In another pan, heat the stock and butter. Slowly add cornmeal to the stock mixture, stirring constantly until thick. Add onion/spice mixture, cheese, salt, and pepper to the cornmeal. Stir until cheese melts. Pour into a buttered baking dish. Bake 20–25 minutes. SERVES 4–6.

Vegetarian Curry

Curried rice:

2	cups water
1	cup rice
¼	teaspoon curry powder
⅓	cup currants
⅓	cup chopped walnuts

Bring the water to a boil. Add the rice, curry powder, currants, and walnuts. Stir to mix. Cover; cook over low heat for 20 minutes or until liquid is absorbed.

Vegetable mixture:

1	cup vegetable broth
1	teaspoon curry powder
½	teaspoon salt
2	cups bite-sized pieces cauliflower
¼	cup sliced mushrooms
½	red pepper, cut into bite-sized pieces
1	mild onion, cut into bite-sized pieces
¼	cup broccoli flowerettes
1	cup sliced zucchini
1	cup green peas
1	tablespoon cornstarch
1	tablespoon water

Mix broth, curry powder, and salt; add the vegetables. Cover, cook over medium-high heat until vegetables are crisp-tender. Drain, reserving liquid. Add water to liquid, if necessary, to make ¾ cup. Place liquid in another pan. Mix cornstarch and 1 tablespoon of water. Add to the ¾ cup of liquid. Stir over medium heat until slightly thickened. Pour over vegetables. Mix gently; serve over curried rice. SERVES 2–4.

The Cat Who Saw Stars

*T*alk about an exciting July! There's the dog-cart race, a Sand Giant, the disappearance of a backpacker, the mystery of the petroglyphs, and what's this about UFOs? Koko is spending a lot of time on the porch at night. What does he see?

Sunny Daze Dinner

Butternut and Roasted Pepper Soup

Coddled Pork Chops

Twice-Baked Potatoes

Broccoli Soufflé

Old-Fashioned Waldorf Salad

Black Forest Cake

🐾

Riker said, "Why don't you come and have dinner with us tonight? The Comptons will be there, and Mildred is doing her famous coddled pork chops."

"What time?"

"About seven."

. . . He [Qwilleran] *walked along the shore to the Rikers' beach house. Most of the cottagers were on their decks, and they waved at Qwilleran; some invited him up for a drink. Last in the row was the Rikers' cottage, a yellow frame bungalow called* SUNNY DAZE.

When Mildred invited them indoors to the table and they were spooning **butternut and roasted pepper soup**, *she asked, "Is everyone going to the Fryers Club play?"*

Butternut and Roasted Pepper Soup

3   red peppers
2   tablespoons chopped onion
2   tablespoons butter or margarine
3   tablespoons all-purpose flour
3   cups light cream
¼   teaspoon garlic powder
salt and pepper to taste
3   tablespoons chopped butternuts or pecans

Put peppers under broiler or over gas flame and broil, turning often, until blistered. Seal in a plastic bag for 5 minutes; peel and cut into small pieces. Place the onion and peppers in a blender and blend until smooth. In a saucepan, melt the butter or margarine. Add the flour and stir until flour is blended into the butter. Slowly add the cream and stir over low heat until thickened. Add the blended pepper mixture, garlic powder, salt, and pepper. Simmer 15 minutes over low heat. Add nuts just before serving. SERVES 4–6.

With the coddled chops were twice-baked potatoes . . .

Coddled Pork Chops

4–6 pork chops, one-inch thick
½ cup all-purpose flour
⅓ cup cooking oil
2 cups apple juice
2 small onions, chopped
4 carrots, sliced
¼ teaspoon dried rosemary
½ teaspoon salt
¼ teaspoon pepper

Preheat oven to 325°. Coat the pork chops with flour. Heat the oil in a skillet. Brown the pork chops and place them in a baking dish. Mix the apple juice, onions, carrots, rosemary, salt, and pepper. Pour over pork chops. Bake 1 hour, covered, or until pork chops are tender. SERVES 4–6.

Twice-Baked Potatoes

---

4 medium baking potatoes
½ cup milk or sour cream
2 tablespoons butter or margarine

salt and pepper to taste
shredded cheddar cheese
chopped chives (optional)

Preheat oven to 425°. Scrub potatoes and dry. Bake 45 to 60 minutes or until soft when pricked with a fork. Cut potatoes in half lengthwise. Carefully scoop the pulp from each potato and place into a mixing bowl. Mash with milk or sour cream, butter or margarine, salt, and pepper. Put the mashed potato back into the shells and place them in a shallow baking dish or on a cookie sheet. Bake approximately 15 minutes. Sprinkle cheddar cheese on top and bake several more minutes until cheese melts. Sprinkle with chives, if desired. SERVES 4–6.

. . . a broccoli soufflé, a pinot noir, and a toast from Lyle Compton: "Thursday's Independence Day! Let's drink to the genius who single-handedly dragged the Fourth of July parade from the pits and launched it to the stars!"

Broccoli Soufflé

⅓   cup finely chopped onion
2   small cloves garlic, minced
3   tablespoons butter or margarine
¼   cup all-purpose flour
½   teaspoon salt
¼   teaspoon pepper
½   teaspoon dried basil
1   cup milk or light cream
1¼   cups shredded cheddar cheese
1   cup chopped cooked broccoli
3   eggs, separated

Preheat oven to 350°. Sauté the onion and garlic in butter or margarine until translucent. Add the flour, salt, pepper, and basil. Slowly add the milk or light cream, stirring until thickened. Place the cheese and broccoli in a large bowl and stir the sauce into them. Cool slightly. Beat the egg yolks and add to cooled broccoli mixture. Beat egg whites until stiff and fold into the broccoli mixture. Place into greased soufflé dish. Bake about 45 minutes or until toothpick inserted in center comes out clean. Serve immediately. SERVES 4.

After an old-fashioned Waldorf salad . . .

Old-Fashioned Waldorf Salad

4 cups unpeeled and chopped apples
½ cup chopped celery
½ cup chopped walnuts
½ cup raisins
½ cup halved grapes
1 teaspoon lemon juice
½ cup mayonnaise
½ cup whipping cream, partially whipped

Mix apples, celery, walnuts, raisins, and grapes together. Add lemon juice, mayonnaise, and cream. Chill. SERVES 8–10.

. . . and Black Forest cake, *and coffee, Lyle wanted to smoke a cigar,*
and the other two men accompanied him down the sandladder to the beach.

Black Forest Cake

Cake:

½	cup shortening
1½	cups sugar
½	cup cocoa
2	egg yolks
1	teaspoon vanilla extract
2	cups milk
2½	cups all-purpose flour
1	teaspoon salt
1	teaspoon baking powder
1½	teaspoons baking soda

Preheat oven to 350°. Cream the shortening and sugar. Add the cocoa, egg yolks, vanilla extract, and 3 tablespoons of the milk. Beat at medium speed for 3–4 minutes. Sift or mix the flour, salt, baking powder, and baking soda together. Beat dry ingredients into the sugar mixture, alternating with the rest of the milk. Pour into two 9-inch greased and floured cake pans. Bake for 30 minutes or until center of cake springs back when touched lightly. Allow cake to cool in pans for about 10 minutes. Turn out onto wire racks to finish cooling.

Kirsch syrup: (optional)

⅓	cup water
¼	cup sugar
2	tablespoons kirsch

$\mathcal{B}oil$ sugar and water 5 minutes. Add kirsch. After cake layers are cool, prick with a fork and brush the syrup over the layers.

$\mathcal{F}illing$:

    1   15-ounce can of dark sweet cherries
    1½   tablespoons cornstarch

$\mathcal{D}rain$ cherries, reserving ⅔ cup of the juice. Place the cherries, reserved juice, and cornstarch in a pan. Cook over medium heat, stirring the entire time, until thickened. Chill.

$\mathcal{F}rosting$:

    ⅓   cup butter or margarine, softened
    ½   cup cocoa
    4½   cups powdered sugar
    ¼   cup milk
    2   teaspoons vanilla extract

$\mathcal{B}eat$ butter or margarine until fluffy. Add cocoa and half the sugar. Beat well. Add the milk and vanilla extract; beat. Add the rest of the sugar and, if necessary, more milk to make frosting easier to spread.

$\mathcal{A}ssembly\ of\ cake$:

After cake is completely cool and filling is chilled, place one layer on a cake plate. Make a ring of frosting around the outer edge of the layer about 1-inch high and ¾-inch wide to hold the cherry filling in place. Spread the filling inside the frosting border. Put the second layer on top. Finish frosting the cake. Garnish with dollops of whipped cream or whipped topping, if desired. SERVES 8–10.

À La Carte

Before going home, he drove out to Fishport to see Doris Hawley—for several reasons . . . A homemade sign on the lawn—a square of plywood nailed to a post—said HOME-BAKES. *That meant muffins, cinnamon rolls, and cookies. Mrs. Hawley was watering the extensive flower garden when Qwilleran pulled into the side drive . . . "What can I do for you?"* [asked Mrs. Hawley]

*"Do you happen to have any **cinnamon rolls**?"* [asked Qwilleran]

Cinnamon Rolls

----

2 tablespoons shortening
3 tablespoons sugar
1 cup sour cream
⅛ teaspoon baking soda
2 eggs
3 cups + ½ cup all-purpose flour
1 package dry yeast, dissolved in ¼ cup warm water (105–115°)
¼ cup butter or margarine, softened
¼ cup sugar
¼ cup brown sugar, packed
1 tablespoon cinnamon

Cream shortening and 3 tablespoons sugar together. Add sour cream, baking soda, eggs, and 3 cups of flour. Stir in softened yeast. Knead in the remaining ½ cup of flour. Dough will be very soft. Place in a greased bowl and then turn the dough over to grease the top. Cover with cloth and let rise until doubled in size, approximately 1 hour. Punch down. Place dough on floured surface and roll to ¼ inch in thickness and 12-inch by 15-inches in size. Spread with butter or margarine. Mix the sugars and cinnamon and sprinkle onto the buttered dough. Roll dough jelly-roll fashion lengthwise. Cut into slices about 1½ inches thick. Place in greased 9-inch by 13-inch pan. Cover. Let rise until doubled in size, approximately 45 minutes. Bake at 350° for 20 minutes or until brown. Allow to cool slightly. Drizzle frosting over warm rolls. MAKES ABOUT 1½ DOZEN ROLLS.

Frosting:

1 cup powdered sugar
2 tablespoons milk
⅛ teaspoon vanilla extract

To make frosting, mix powdered sugar with milk to make a drizzling consistency. Add vanilla extract.

They [Alice Ogilvie and Qwill] *sat around a corner of the big table for* *coffee and* doughnuts. *They were real fried-cakes, prepared that morning because Alice was taking them to a coffee hour at the church. Qwilleran had to control his enthusiasm and downright greed.*

Alice's Fried Cakes

—————

1   square semi-sweet baking chocolate, melted
1   cup + ½ cup sugar
1   egg
½   cup cream
1   cup sour cream
½   teaspoon salt
2   teaspoons soda
½   teaspoon nutmeg
3½   cups all-purpose flour
shortening

Melt chocolate according to package directions. Set aside. Cream the 1 cup sugar and egg. Stir in the cream and sour cream. While stirring, drizzle the warm melted chocolate into the cool sour cream mixture. Chocolate will harden into small flecks. In a separate bowl, sift or mix the salt, soda, nutmeg, and flour together. Add the flour mixture to the sour cream mixture. Beat well. On a floured surface, pat or roll out dough to about ¼ inch in thickness. Dough will be soft. Cut into squares. Fry in shortening over medium-high heat or in a deep fryer at 365° until brown on both sides. Remove from oil and drain on paper towels. Cool slightly; roll in the ½ cup sugar. MAKES ABOUT 3 DOZEN.

*"Dinner is served," Mildred announced. It was squash bisque, **lamb stew**, crusty bread, and green salad. Dessert and coffee were served on the deck, during which Qwilleran and Arch entertained them with a tell-all session about growing up in Chicago.*

Skillet Lamb Stew

2   pounds lamb, diced
⅓   cup (approximate) + 2 tablespoons all-purpose flour
oil
½   teaspoon salt
¼   teaspoon pepper
water + ⅓ cup water
6   medium potatoes, cut into small pieces
6   carrots, sliced
8–10   pearl onions
1   cup fresh peas
3   medium tomatoes, diced

Place lamb and ⅓ cup flour in a plastic or paper bag and shake to coat. Remove from bag and brown in oil in large skillet. Season with salt and pepper. Cover with water. Simmer about an hour or until nearly tender. Add vegetables, except tomatoes. Simmer 30 minutes. Add tomatoes, simmer 10 minutes longer. Mix remaining flour and ⅓ cup water. Stir into stew and cook until thickened. SERVES 6.

All went well that evening: Qwilleran thought the lamb shank superb; Tess loved the play. Afterward, he served **sangria** *on the lake porch and said, "Tess, your visit has been memorable!"*

Sangria

---

ice cubes
¾ ounce orange juice
¾ ounce lemon juice
½ ounce corn syrup
4 ounces red wine
2 ounces club soda

Place ice cubes in a large glass. Pour the rest of the ingredients over the ice and stir.

The Cat Who Robbed a Bank

The old Pickax Hotel opens again with a new name, new furniture, and even a new chef. Everyone in town is thrilled until one of the first hotel guests is murdered in his bed. Koko, the cat who knows his Shakespeare, tries to give Qwilleran clues.

New Century Dining
at the Mackintosh Inn

Curried Chicken Liver Crêpe

🐾

Eggplant and Avocado Tartlet

🐾

Deviled Crab

🐾

Spinach Salad

🐾

Desserts

Polly thought she could make a meal of four savories and a salad—and no dessert. She would have a toasted cheese roulade, a curried chicken liver crêpe, eggplant and avocado tartlet with cashews, and deviled crab on the half shell. Her salad would be baby spinach leaves, mandarin orange slices, and crumbled Stilton with a tomato vinaigrette dressing.

There were desserts—rum cake, lemon soufflé, chocolate praline cheesecake, blackberry cobbler—and then it was over.

Curried Chicken Liver Crêpe

Crêpes:

1	cup all-purpose flour
⅛	teaspoon salt
2	eggs
1	cup milk
1	tablespoon + 1 tablespoon vegetable oil

Place flour and salt in a mixing bowl. Mix the eggs until yolks and whites are blended. Add the milk and 1 tablespoonful of the oil. Slowly add the milk mixture to the flour and salt, stirring until smooth. Heat the other tablespoonful of oil in a crêpe pan or skillet and pour it out. Pour in enough batter to cover the bottom of the skillet. Cook over medium heat until the edges of the crêpe are dry. Turn it over and cook the other side 15–20 seconds. Continue with the rest of the batter. Stack with pieces of oiled waxed paper between each crêpe.

Crêpe Filling:

- ½ pound chicken livers
- 2 tablespoons butter or margarine
- 1 hard-boiled egg
- 1 8-ounce package cream cheese
- 1 tablespoon finely chopped dried parsley
- ½ teaspoon curry powder
- ½ teaspoon salt
- ⅛ teaspoon pepper
- 3 tablespoons melted butter or margarine

Preheat oven to 350°. Fry the livers in the butter or margarine over medium heat until they are no longer pink in the center—about 15 minutes. Place the livers and egg in a food processor and process until finely chopped. Add the cream cheese a little at a time, along with the parsley, curry powder, salt, and pepper. When the mixture is smooth, place about 2 tablespoonsful on each crêpe and roll up. Place in a buttered baking dish, with the seam-side down. Drizzle with melted butter. Bake 15 minutes. MAKES 12–15 CRÊPES.

Eggplant and Avocado Tartlet

- 1 15-ounce box piecrusts
- 1 cup peeled, cubed eggplant
- 3 tablespoons chopped onion
- 1 clove garlic, finely chopped
- ½ cup water
- 2 eggs, well-beaten
- 2 slices bread, torn into small pieces
- ½ cup milk
- 1 cup peeled, cubed avocado
- ⅓ cup coarsley chopped cashews

1½   cups shredded cheddar cheese
1   teaspoon salt
⅛   teaspoon pepper

Preheat oven to 350°. Unfold the 2 piecrusts and place half of each crust in each of 4 individual serving, size baking dishes. Put aside and simmer the eggplant, onion, and garlic in the ½ cup water until the eggplant is tender; drain. Combine the eggs, bread, milk, avocado, cashews, 1 cup of the cheese, salt, and pepper with the eggplant mixture. Pour into the crust-lined dishes. Bake for 30 minutes. Then sprinkle with the remaining ½ cup cheese and bake until the cheese melts. SERVES 4.

Deviled Crab

½   cup + 2 tablespoons butter or margarine, melted, cooled
¼   cup cream
1½   teaspoons dry mustard
⅛   teaspoon cayenne pepper
2   6-ounce cans crabmeat
1   cup finely chopped celery
1   cup finely chopped onion
2   tablespoons finely chopped green bell pepper
2   tablespoons finely chopped dried parsley
1½   cups crushed saltine crackers

Preheat oven to 350°. Brush 2 tablespoons of the melted butter over the sides and bottom of a 1½-quart baking dish or half shells. Mix the ½ cup butter, cream, mustard, and cayenne pepper in a medium-sized bowl until the mustard has dissolved. Add the crabmeat, celery, onions, green pepper, parsley, and cracker crumbs and mix well. Put the mixture into the baking dish or the half shells. Bake 30 minutes if the mixture is in a dish, 15 minutes if in half shells or until the top is browned. SERVES 4–6.

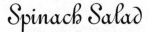

Spinach Salad

1 bunch or package baby spinach leaves
2 11-ounce cans mandarin oranges
4 tablespoons sunflower seeds
Stilton cheese, crumbled
1 recipe tomato vinaigrette salad dressing

Thoroughly wash the spinach leaves. Gently dry and arrange on 4 salad plates. Drain mandarin oranges and place them on the spinach leaves. Sprinkle each serving with 1 tablespoonful of sunflower seeds and cheese to taste. Serve with tomato vinaigrette dressing.

Tomato Vinaigrette Dressing:

1 tablespoon cider vinegar
1 tablespoon fresh lemon juice
¼ teaspoon dry mustard
¼ teaspoon salt
pepper to taste
½ cup canola oil
1 tablespoon olive oil
1 tomato, peeled, seeded, and diced into very small pieces

Place vinegar, lemon juice, mustard, salt, pepper, and 2 tablespoons of the diced tomato into blender and blend until salt has dissolved. Add oil slowly, blending constantly. When well-mixed, stir in 3–4 additional tablespoonsful of tomato. Do not blend after addition of final tomato pieces. SERVES 4.

Rum Cake

Cake:

6	eggs
1	cup granulated sugar
1	teaspoon vanilla
1	cup all-purpose flour
½	cup cocoa powder
½	cup melted butter

Preheat oven to 350°. Place the eggs in a double boiler. Stir over simmering water until warm. Remove from heat and place in mixing bowl with sugar. With electric mixer, beat 6 minutes at medium speed. Increase speed and beat until mixture stands in soft peaks; about 5 minutes. Add vanilla. Mix flour and cocoa powder. Fold into egg mixture. Add melted butter. Pour into 2 greased and floured 9-inch cake pans. Bake 35–40 minutes. Turn out on rack at once to cool.

Rum Syrup:

1	cup sugar
½	cup water
3	tablespoons rum, Haitian or dark Jamaican

Place sugar and water in saucepan and bring to a boil over medium heat. Stir occasionally to dissolve sugar. Cover and allow to cool. Add rum. Brush on tops of cooled cake layers. Cake should be moist but not soggy. All the syrup may not be used.

Filling:

2	ounces chocolate
2	teaspoons butter
3	tablespoons cream
½	teaspoon vanilla
1	cup confectioners' sugar

Melt chocolate and butter over very low heat. Remove from heat and stir in cream. Slowly add vanilla and enough of the sugar to make a filling of spreading consistency. Spread over the top of one cake layer, which has been brushed with syrup. Place the other layer on top. Do not frost top layer.

Topping:

    1   12-ounce bag semi-sweet chocolate chips
    1   cup whipping cream
    2   tablespoons rum, Haitian or dark Jamaican
    chocolate sprinkles

Place chocolate chips and cream in a double boiler over medium heat. Stir constantly until chocolate melts. Remove from heat and stir in rum. Pour the mixture over the cake after it has thickened but before it has set. Decorate with chocolate sprinkles. SERVES 12.

Lemon Soufflé

    1½   cups milk
    ½   cup sugar
    ¼   cup butter
    ⅓   cup all-purpose flour
    ½   cup lemon juice
    1   teaspoon grated lemon rind
    6   stiffly beaten egg whites

Preheat oven to 425°. Place milk and sugar in small pan; bring to boil. Remove from heat. Melt butter in double boiler. Add flour and stir to a smooth consistency. Gradually pour milk mixture into flour paste. Stir constantly and cook until thickened. Add lemon juice and lemon rind. Put mixture into a mixing bowl. Allow to cool slightly. Whisk in approximately ⅓ of the egg whites; add remaining whites and mix thoroughly. Pour into buttered 7-inch soufflé dish. Place dish 1 shelf above center of oven. Bake 30 minutes. Serve immediately. SERVES 4.

Chocolate Praline Cheesecake

Crust:
- 1⅔ cups crushed graham crackers
- ¼ cup sugar
- 6 tablespoons melted butter or margarine

Mix crumbs, sugar, and butter thoroughly. Press into bottom and sides of 10-inch springform pan.

Cheesecake Filling:
- 1 12-ounce bag semi-sweet chocolate chips
- 4 8-ounce packages cream cheese
- 2 cups sugar
- 4 eggs
- 1 teaspoon cocoa
- 1 teaspoon vanilla extract
- 1 16-ounce carton sour cream

Preheat oven to 300°. Put chocolate chips in top of double boiler. Simmer over low heat until chocolate melts. Beat cream cheese with an electric beater until it is fluffy. Add sugar a little at a time, mixing after each addition. Add eggs, one at a time, beating well after each egg. Lower the speed of the mixer and add the melted chocolate, cocoa, and vanilla extract. Blend in the sour cream and pour the mixture into the graham cracker crust. Bake for 1 hour and 35 minutes. Cool; chill for 8–10 hours before serving.

Praline Topping:

- ¼ cup butter or margarine
- 1¼ cups brown sugar, firmly packed
- ¾ cup light corn syrup
- 3 tablespoons all-purpose flour
- 1 5-ounce can evaporated milk
- 1 cup chopped pecans

Place butter or margarine, brown sugar, corn syrup, and flour in a saucepan over medium heat. Stir until butter is melted. Bring the mixture to a boil, then reduce heat to low and cook approximately 5 minutes, stirring constantly. Remove from heat and let cool until lukewarm. Stir in evaporated milk and pecans. Pour over individual slices of cheesecake. SERVES 12.

Blackberry Cobbler

Fruit:

- 4 cups fresh or frozen blackberries
- 6 tablespoons sugar
- 3 tablespoons cornstarch
- 2 tablespoons butter or margarine

Preheat oven to 400°. Butter an 8-inch square baking dish. Combine the berries, sugar, and cornstarch in a large bowl. Place in the baking dish. Dot with butter. Bake until mixture begins to bubble; about 15 minutes. Stir gently.

Crust:

- 1 cup all-purpose flour
- 2 tablespoons sugar
- ¼ teaspoon salt
- 2 teaspoons baking powder

❧ *The Cat Who Robbed a Bank* ❧

¼ cup butter or margarine
1–2 tablespoons milk
1 egg
½ teaspoon sugar

Mix flour, sugar, salt, and baking powder. Cut the butter or margarine into the flour mixture until crumbly. Beat 1 tablespoon milk and egg together; add to flour mixture. If necessary, add additional milk. The dough should be stiff. On a floured surface, pat out the dough to about ½ inch in thickness. Cut into squares and place on top of hot berries. Sprinkle with sugar. Bake 10–15 minutes or until biscuits are brown and fruit is bubbling around the edges. SERVES 6.

À La Carte

"A bright young woman in an embroidered vest served them *baba ghanouj* and spanokopetes, and he [Qwilleran] said, "I wish my mother could see me now—eating spinach and eggplant. And liking it!"

Baba Ghanouj

1 medium-sized eggplant
1 small onion, chopped into large pieces
1 small clove garlic
1¼ cup lemon juice
1 tablespoon olive oil
1 teaspoon salt
broccoli, cauliflower, carrots, celery, green peppers, and green onions cut into dipping size

Preheat oven to 400°. Prick eggplant on all sides with fork. Bake 40 minutes. Let cool, peel, and cut into small pieces. Put eggplant, onion, garlic, lemon juice, oil, and salt in food processor or blender. Process until smooth. Serve with vegetables for dipping.

Celia laughed happily. She always laughed at the mildest quip from "the Chief." She explained, "I've brought you two meals of **macaroni and cheese** *and a two-pound meat loaf."*

Celia's Macaroni and Cheese

8	ounces elbow macaroni, uncooked
1	small onion, chopped
1	small green pepper, chopped
1	10¾-ounce can tomato soup
⅔	cup shredded cheddar cheese
¾	cup processed American cheese, melted
¾	cup crushed crackers
¼	cup melted butter or margarine

Preheat oven to 350°. Cook macaroni according to package directions. Drain macaroni. Stir onion, green pepper, tomato soup, cheddar cheese, and processed cheese into macaroni. Place mixture in buttered baking dish. Mix crackers and butter or margarine and sprinkle on top. Bake, uncovered, until crackers begin to brown, approximately 30 minutes. SERVES 6.

"Whaddaya want?" came a demanding voice [Lois] through the pass-through window.

"Apple pie and a cuppa!" he [Qwilleran] shouted back.

"Apple's all gone! You can have cherry."

He had to admit the pie was good—not too tart, not too sweet, not too gelatinous, not too soupy.

Lois's Cherry Pie

Pastry:
- 1 cup all-purpose flour
- ½ cup quick-cooking oatmeal
- ½ cup shortening
- 1 teaspoon salt
- 4–6 tablespoons ice water

Mix the flour, oatmeal, and salt together. Cut in shortening until the mixture is the size of small peas. Add water a tablespoonful at a time, mixing lightly with a fork, until the mixture holds together. Roll out on a lightly floured surface. Place in an 8-inch pie pan.

Cherry filling:
- 1 14½-ounce can red tart cherries (pitted), not drained
- 1 cup sugar
- 6 tablespoons cornstarch
- ½ cup cold water

Preheat oven to 350°. Place the undrained cherries in a saucepan. Add sugar and heat. In a small bowl, mix the water and cornstarch. Add it to the cherries. Stir over medium heat until thickened. Pour the mixture into the unbaked piecrust. Sprinkle with topping. Bake for 35–40 minutes.

Topping:

- ¾ cup all-purpose flour
- 1 cup quick-cooking oatmeal
- ½ cup brown sugar
- 6 tablespoons butter or margarine
- ½ cup chopped pecans

Mix flour, oatmeal, and brown sugar. Cut in butter or margarine until mixture is crumbly. Add nuts.

"I'm making beef pot pies today. Shall I make an extra one for you?"
[asked Celia]

Beef Pot Pie

- 1¼ pounds stew meat
- ¼ cup all-purpose flour
- 3 tablespoons cooking oil
- 1 teaspoon salt
- ¼ teaspoon pepper
- water
- 1 bay leaf
- 1 14½-ounce can beef broth
- 2 cups sliced carrots

          3 cups cubed potatoes
          1 cup chopped onion
          ⅓ cup finely chopped celery
          2 cups sliced fresh mushrooms

Cut meat into bite-sized pieces. Place meat and flour in a plastic bag; shake to coat. Heat oil in a stockpot. Remove meat from bag of flour and brown it in the oil. Season with salt and pepper. Cover the meat with water. Cover pan and simmer until nearly tender (about 2 hours). Add additional water, if necessary. Add bay leaf, beef broth, and vegetables. Increase heat to medium and cook until vegetables are tender (about 1 hour). Remove bay leaf. Place meat mixture in a 9-inch by 13-inch baking dish. Cool slightly. Top with crust.

Crust:

          2 cups all-purpose flour
          1 teaspoon salt
          1 tablespoon dried parsley
          ⅔ cup shortening
        4–6 tablespoons ice water

Preheat oven to 425°. Mix flour, salt, and parsley. Cut in shortening until mixture resembles small peas. Add water a tablespoonful at a time until the dough holds together. Roll out on a floured surface into a 10-inch by 14-inch rectangle. Cover the slightly cooled beef mixture with the crust, crimping the dough to the edges of the baking dish on all sides. Cut slits in dough to allow steam to escape. Bake for 20 minutes or until crust is lightly browned. SERVES 6.

Feline Fare

FROM THE PANTRY

On the way home he stopped at Toodles' Market to buy the Siamese something to eat—always a problem because they had fickle palates. Their preferences changed just often enough to keep him perpetually on his toes. There was only one constant: no cat food! As if they could read labels, they disdained any product intended for the four-legged trade. (The Cat Who Wasn't There)

As Qwilleran opened a can of red salmon, crushed the bones with a fork, removed the black skin, and arranged it on two plates, he thought, Cats don't fight for their rights; they take them for granted. They have a right to be fed, watered, stroked on demand, and supplied with a lap and a clean commode . . . and if they don't get their rights, they quietly commit certain acts of civil disobedience . . . Tyrants! . . . The two gobbling heads were so intent on their salmon that even the loud bell of the kitchen phone failed to disturb them. (The Cat Who Blew the Whistle)

The following foods are what you will need to keep on hand to feed cats with such discriminating feline palates as those possessed by Koko and Yum Yum. Individual cans of these foods are good, but cases of cans are much better—just ask Koko.

- Boned chicken
- Caviar
- Cocktail shrimp
- Corned beef
- Crabmeat, Alaskan (serve with goat cheese)

- Red salmon
- Smoked oysters
- White grape juice
- White tuna, solid pack

FROM THE REFRIGERATOR

"What would you like for breakfast? Turkey from the deli? Or cocktail shrimp from a can?"

Koko was not present to cast his vote, but Yum Yum was rubbing against Qwilleran's ankles in anticipation and curling her tail lovingly around his leg, and he knew she preferred turkey. He began to mince slices of white meat. (The Cat Who Went Underground)

Some foods would spoil in the pantry, so you'll need to reserve a shelf in the refrigerator for your feline friends.

- Deli corned beef
- Deli turkey
- Feta cheese
- Gruyère cheese
- Havarti cheese
- Ice cream, French vanilla
- Lobster
- Off-the-bird turkey

- Oysters
- Pot roast
- Roast beef
- Round steak
- Roquefort cheese
- Smoked salmon
- Tenderloin tip

. . . His diet is simple. There is raw beef in the refrigerator. You merely carve it in small pieces the size of a lima bean, put it in a pan with a little broth, and warm it gently. A dash of salt and a sprinkling of sage or thyme will be appreciated. (The Cat Who Could Read Backwards)

Then the cat led the way into the kitchen with exalted tail and starched gait to supervise the preparation of his dinner. With his whiskers curved down in anticipation, he sat on the drainboard and watched the chopping of chicken livers, the slow cooking in butter, the addition of cream, and the dash of curry powder. (The Cat Who Turned On and Off)

If your cat is not in the mood to eat something out of a can tonight, you might try one of these "catcipes" to delight your gourmand.

- Alaska king crab and raw egg yolk, garnished with English cheddar
- Beef cooked in broth, a dash of salt, sprinkled with sage or thyme
- Canned crabmeat garnished with goat cheese
- Chopped fresh beef and canned consommé
- Chunks of beef tenderloin with thin gravy
- Curried chicken
- Diced round steak
- Livers sautéed in butter with cream and a dash of curry
- Minced beef with cottage cheese, laced with tomato sauce
- Minced lamb with juice
- Red salmon garnished with a smoked oyster
- Sardines with cheese sauce, vitamin drops, and crumbled egg yolks
- Sautéed chicken livers with a garnish of egg yolk and bacon crumbles
- Veal kidneys in cream
- Veal stroganoff

FROM RESTAURANTS

When Derek finally arrived with the shrimp timbales in lobster puree, he apologized for being late and said, "The chef wants to know how they liked the veal blanquette yesterday."

"Okay, except for the Japanese mushrooms, Derek. They don't like Japanese mushrooms. And tell him not to send marinated artichoke hearts—only fresh ones. Their favorite food is turkey, but it must be off-the-bird—not that rolled stuff." (The Cat Who Sniffed Glue)

When the cats can't go to the restaurants, the restaurants come to them.

- Boiled lobster tail (Fish Tank Restaurant)
- Chicken liver pâté and boned frog legs (Old Stone Mill)
- Ham (Lois's Luncheonette)
- Meatballs (Lois's Luncheonette)
- Minced baked shrimp stuffed with lump crabmeat (Roberto's)
- Poached salmon with capers (Old Stone Mill)
- Shrimp timbales in lobster puree (Old Stone Mill)
- Turkey off-the-bird (Press Club)
- Veal blanquette (Old Stone Mill)
- Veal, scallops, and squid (Roberto's)

FROM FRIENDS

"How often are the cats fed?"

"Morning and evening, plus a handful of your crunchy cereal at noon and bedtime. You'll find canned and frozen delicacies for them in the kitchen."

"To tell the truth, I'd rather cook for them" Mildred said. *"I really would!"* (The Cat Who Wasn't There)

When all else fails, a feline knows that friends will come through. Koko and Yum Yum have plenty of friends from the looks of the list below.

- Cereal (Mildred Hanstable Riker)
- Hagis (Brodie)
- Kabibbles (Celia Robinson)
- Liver pâté (Dolly Lessmore)
- Meatballs (Vickie Bushland)
- Meat loaf (Mildred Hanstable Riker)
- Minced baked shrimp stuffed with lump crabmeat (Robert Maus, aka Roberto)
- Pot roast with pan juices, grated carrot, sprinkling of hard-cooked egg yolks (Iris Cobb)
- Pork liver cupcakes (Hixie Rice)
- Salmon mousse (Mildred Hanstable Riker)

FROM THE BARN

"We have a colony of fruit flies that came with the apple barn, and they come out of hibernation at this time of year. Koko catches them on the wing and munches them as hors d'oeuvres." (The Cat Who Wasn't There)

There's just no way to explain a cat's preferences!

- Fruit flies

Metric Equivalents and Cooking Temperatures

METRIC EQUIVALENTS

VOLUME

Slightly less than ¼ teaspoon	1 ml
Slightly less than ½ teaspoon	2 ml
1 teaspoon	5 ml
1 tablespoon	15 ml
1 tablespoon plus 2 teaspoons	25 ml
⅛ cup	30 ml
¼ cup minus 2 teaspoons	50 ml
¼ cup	60 ml
⅓ cup	80 ml
½ cup	125 ml
⅔ cup	160 ml
¾ cup	180 ml
1 cup	250 ml
1 pint plus 2 tablespoons	500 ml
1 quart plus ¼ cup	1 liter

SOLIDS

1 ounce plus a large pinch	30 g
¼ pound	125 g
½ pound plus less than an ounce	250 g

		500 g
1 pound plus 1⅔ ounces		500 g
1½ pounds plus about 2½ ounces		750 g
2 pounds plus about 3½ ounces		1000 g (1 kg)
1 cup all-purpose flour (about 4 ounces)		about 112 g
1 cup granulated sugar (about 8 ounces)		about 224 g
8 tablespoons butter (4 ounces = 1 stick)		125 g

COOKING TEMPERATURES

DEGREES CELSIUS		DEGREES FAHRENHEIT	GAS MARK
150	Slow oven	300	2
158	Slow oven	325	3
177	Moderate oven	350	4
190	Moderately hot oven	375	5
204	Hot oven	400	6
214	Hot oven	425	7
232	Very hot oven	450	8
260	Very hot oven	500	9

Index